THE LONDON

Ritz

BOOK OF

Breakfasts

EPIGRAPH:

'*A man of taste is seen at once in the array of his breakfast table.*'

Crotchet Castle, Thomas Love Peacock, 1831

THE LONDON

Ritz

BOOK OF

Breakfasts

HELEN SIMPSON

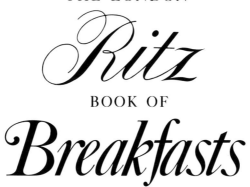

Ebury Press
LONDON

To my grandmother

Published by Ebury Press
Division of
The National Magazine Company Ltd
Colquhoun House
27–37 Broadwick Street
London W1V 1FR

Produced on licence for
Ritz Products (UK) Ltd

First impression 1988

ISBN 0 85223 664 6

Edited by Susan Ward
Copy Editor: Norma MacMillan
Art Director: Frank Phillips
Designed by Peartree Design Associates
Illustrated by Dennis and Sheila Curran

Filmset by
Advanced Filmsetters (Glasgow) Ltd
Printed in Great Britain
at the University Press, Cambridge

Acknowledgements
The author would like to thank Nick Gauna
and Roger Sparrow of the Ritz Hotel, London
for their help.

As well as giving recipes for breakfast dishes
served at The Ritz Hotel, London this book
includes many additional ideas. The hotel does
not serve all the dishes for which recipes are
given here.

Note on flour for those using Cup Measures
All-purpose flour can be substituted for cake
flour, although this may not give such fine
results.

Contents

———•———

Breakfast at the Ritz

reakfast at the Ritz is a positive-spirited meal during which the business of the day ahead falls into manageable perspective.

Indeed, it would be difficult to feel less than sanguine in the Ritz's restaurant, a long light room lined with panels of marble as beautiful as their names—Brèche d'Alep, Rose de Norvege and Vert de Suède. Intricate bronze garlands link the chandeliers; puffs of painted cloud drift with trompe l'oeil insouciance across the cerulean ceiling. Through the tall windows can be glimpsed the Ritz's secret garden within Green Park.

Even so, this is no place for mere morning escapists. 'Breakfast is never entirely devoted to pleasure,' asserts the Ritz's head breakfast waiter. 'It generally serves some purpose apart from nourishment. It is an important meal for businessmen especially; I can tell the state of the stock market by its popularity.' Watches flash urgently on the wrists of breakfasters, moon-phased jewelled movements urging their owners on to do battle with the bears and bulls of the City or the lions and unicorns of Whitehall. Sometimes, a group of whey-faced revellers in satin and taffeta close a night on the town with kedgeree and black coffee, or a tender couple, mindful of the adage that 'The critical period in matrimony is breakfast-time', celebrate their anniversary here over a pair of kippers. But mostly this is the meal for those whose time is precious.

A serious breakfaster waves his company

report above the silver toast-rack, the poached white peaches, the grilled kidneys and the brioches. His trenchant voice falls softly into the Empyrean air. He will leave for his day of air-conditioned efficiency fuelled and sleeked by breakfasting under the gaze of the Ritz's bronze river god, fortified by his brush with the utes and Pan-pipes, the painted stag, the toppling silver-pink roses and the distant peacock.

Down in the kitchen, the breakfast shift begins in the smallest hours, starting at three o'clock with the vandyking of ruby grapefruit and the poaching of fruit for compôtes. Pithless Florida cocktails are arranged in glass *coupes*, scores of oranges and grapefruit are squeezed for their juice, and halved melons are filled with strawberries or raspberries. At half-past five the various bowls and jugs of fruit, cereals and juices are taken up to the restaurant. At six, the pastry chef makes the morning's Danish pastries, and half an hour later the muesli is mixed with milk, orange juice, and chopped peeled apples and pears.

Breakfast begins at half-past seven and is served for the next three hours. Tea is rousingly strong: coffee arrives in a silver pot with a silver jug of hot milk. A circular pink-damask-covered banquette, corresponding to the Edwardian sideboard, invites the breakfaster to choose, displaying: platters of the sliced meats and cheeses favoured by Teutonic breakfasters; baskets of croissants, brioches and seed-capped rolls; silver trays of fresh fruit (familiar or tropical according to season) grouped in fans and slices; hard-boiled eggs, wreathed in the damask whorls of a napkin;

banana breakfast bread (a firm favourite with habitual Ritz breakfasters); pots of yoghurt perched on crushed ice floes in silver tureens; half a dozen or more bowls of freshly poached fruit—glossy green figs, apricots, black cherries, Mirabelle plums, prunes, white peaches, and sometimes the renowned Ritz rhubarb, gently stewed in white wine with juniper berries.

And then, of course, those who would not dream of starting the day without a Proper Cooked Breakfast will order from a menu of traditional dishes, including bacon and eggs, grilled kidneys, porridge and kippers, black pudding, Cumberland sausage, scrambled eggs with smoked salmon, and quintessential kedgeree.

KEDGEREE

The Hindi Khichri was a hotchpotch Indian dish of rice boiled with lentils, onions, eggs and spices. The British in India concocted their own version, and smudged its name into kedgeree. Typical is this recipe by the pseudonymous 'Wyvern' in his *Culinary Jottings: a treatise in thirty chapters on Reformed Cookery for Anglo-Indian Exiles*, written in 1885: 'Kegeree (kitchri) of the English type is composed of boiled rice, chopped hard-boiled egg, cold minced fish, and a lump of fresh butter: these are all tossed together in the frying-pan, flavoured with pepper, salt, and any minced garden herb such as cress, parsley, or marjoram, and served smoking hot.'

The Ritz has perfected its own version of this dish. Nick Gauna, Senior Sous-Chef, advises,

'Only use the best oak-smoked haddock in kedgeree, not the dyed yellow-golden version.'

METRIC/IMPERIAL	CUP MEASURES
50 g/2 oz butter	4 tbsp butter
2 onions, sliced	2 onions, sliced
1 small green pepper, seeded and sliced	1 small sweet green pepper, seeded and sliced
1 small courgette, sliced	1 small zucchini, sliced
75 g/3 oz pineapple chunks	$\frac{1}{2}$ cup pineapple chunks
1 small mango, sliced	1 small mango, sliced
10 ml/2 tsp plain flour	2 tsp unbleached flour
10 ml/2 tsp desiccated coconut	2 tsp shredded dried coconut
5 ml/1 tsp mild Madras curry powder	1 tsp mild curry powder
5 ml/1 tsp tomato purée	1 tsp tomato paste
600 ml/1 pint chicken stock	$2\frac{1}{2}$ cups chicken stock
275 g/10 oz long-grain patna rice	$1\frac{1}{2}$ cups long-grain patna rice
4 eggs, hard-boiled and cut into quarters	4 eggs, hard-cooked and cut into quarters
350 g/12 oz smoked haddock fillets, gently poached	$\frac{3}{4}$ lb finnan haddie fillets, gently poached

Serves 4

Melt the butter in a large, heavy-based saucepan. Add the prepared onions, green pepper, courgette or zucchini, pineapple and mango, and cook very gently over a low heat for 10 minutes or so, thickening the mixture by sprinkling over and stirring in the flour. Stir in the coconut, curry powder and tomato purée. Add the chicken stock, a little at a time, and gradually bring to the boil. Turn the heat down and simmer the mixture gently for 30 minutes,

CÉSAR RITZ

César Ritz was born in 1850, the thirteenth child of a Swiss herdsman. He worked his early youth away as a waiter in *prix fixe* restaurants and bars, but his remarkable energy and abilities bore him irrevocably upwards. He managed hotels in Switzerland, Italy and France, transforming each into a centre of fashion by means of his social percipience and imagination. No wonder the press dubbed him 'the persuasive Swiss with the Midas touch'. He was full of zest and courtesy, with a passion for scrupulous cleanliness which was by no means universal among hoteliers at that time. He dressed his moustaches daily with Pomade Hongroise, and always wore a flower in his buttonhole. He went riding for exercise, and ate and drank with epicurean discernment, though sparingly.

D'Oyly Carte was the first to lure him to London, in 1889, to manage his new hotel, the Savoy. Ritz commented, 'He wants the clientèle I can give him.' He brought with him his brilliant chef Georges-Auguste Escoffier. 'Monsieur Escoffier is undoubtedly the finest chef in the world,' declared Ritz. 'He is far in advance of all the other chefs I have ever met.' Soon the cream of London society had deserted its dining rooms and clubs for the hotel where Ritz was now

Manager. 'You know better than I do what I like,' the gourmet Prince of Wales would say. 'Arrange a dinner to my taste.' When Ritz left some ten years later, the prince declared, 'Where Ritz goes, I go.' The Hotel Ritz, designed by the architect Charles Mewès, and proudly described as 'le dernier cri de l'élégance' by its owner, Ritz himself, opened in Paris in 1896 and became the instant centre for *le tout Paris*. Ritz's next venture was the magnificent Carlton Hotel (which stood in the Haymarket, London, where New Zealand House now stands). Soon after the Carlton's opening at the turn of the century, how-ever, Ritz fell ill. The fastidiousness, obsessive attention to detail and per-fectionism which had brought him such dazzling success had also driven him into a nervous decline, and for the remaining sixteen years of his life he was to drag on in a state of twilight collapse.

Soon after Ritz's breakdown, a company of his business associates founded the Ritz Hotel, Piccadilly, ap-pointing his favourite architect, Charles Mewès, along with Mewès' new partner Arthur Davis. The result was a gilded apotheosis of the *belle époque*, shot through with the atmosphere of pleasure and the belief in quality and simplicity which Ritz had brought to all his hotels,

and crowned with his name. Ritz was well enough to attend the hotel's opening party, writing the next morning to the architects that 'everyone admired the hotel, and I must say myself it is superb—it is the prettiest in the world.'

stirring now and then, until the liquid has evaporated. Purée the resulting mixture in a food processor, and keep it hot in a covered basin in a low oven.

Boil the rice as usual, and when it is cooked and drained, spread it evenly over the bottom of a large heated gratin dish or other oval or rectangular serving dish. Arrange the eggs on the rice. Take the poached fish and lightly break it into flakes, carefully discarding skin and bones. Place it around the eggs. Pour the hot curried sauce over so that it covers all the ingredients except the extreme margins of the rice.

Serve very hot at the table, mixing the ingredients rapidly together with two forks just before you spoon the kedgeree on to hot plates.

'The hotelier who cannot learn to keep his own counsel had better choose another métier!' César Ritz

'Ritz, it is easy to see how you learned tact and patience. You learned those lessons herding your father's stupid cattle in the mountain pastures of the Niederwald.' Lillie Langtry

'What a magnificent banquet room this would make!' César Ritz, on entering St Peter's on his first visit to Rome

'Kings and princes will be jealous of you, Ritz. You are going to teach the world how to live.' Henry Higgins, the English lawyer who was Ritz's financial backer at the time of the Paris Ritz's launch

SCRAMBLED EGGS WITH SMOKED SALMON AND CHIVES

——METRIC/IMPERIAL—— •	——CUP MEASURES——
25 g/1 oz butter	2 tbsp butter
4 eggs	4 eggs
75 ml/3 fl oz double cream	6 tbsp heavy cream
salt and white pepper	salt and white pepper
15 g/½ oz smoked salmon, chopped fine	½ oz (about 2 tbsp) smoked salmon, chopped fine
5 ml/1 tsp chives, chopped very fine	1 tsp chives, chopped very fine
25 g/1 oz smoked salmon, sliced into matchstick-thin strips about 5 cm/2 inches long	1 oz smoked salmon, sliced into matchstick-thin strips about 2 inches long
2 slices crustless brown toast, buttered	2 slices crustless brown toast, buttered
100 g/4 oz smoked salmon slices	¼ lb smoked salmon slices
2 small tomatoes	2 small tomatoes

Serves 2

Heat the butter in a heavy-based saucepan until it starts to foam. Beat the eggs and cream together with a fork, adding a pinch of salt and the same of pepper. Move the pan to a low heat, pour in the egg mixture, and shift the swiftly-forming egg curds gently around the pan with a wooden spoon until they look creamy and almost (but not quite) cooked.

Remove from the heat. Stir in the chopped smoked salmon and the chives. Spoon these emerald and coral-flecked curds on to the slice of toast on each plate, and arrange a lattice of fine strips of smoked salmon on top of each mound of egg. Arrange a swathe of sliced smoked salmon around each latticed mound, place a quartered tomato on one side of the plate, and serve.

This dish is served at the Ritz with a half-lemon tied in muslin.

BANANA BREAKFAST BREAD

——METRIC/IMPERIAL—— •	——CUP MEASURES——
75 g/3 oz butter	6 tbsp butter
175 g/6 oz caster sugar	⅞ cup sugar
2 eggs	2 eggs
275 g/10 oz ripe bananas	10 oz ripe bananas (2 small)
225 g/8 oz plain flour	1¾ cups unbleached flour
2.5 ml/½ tsp salt	½ tsp salt
15 ml/1 tbsp baking powder	1 tbsp baking powder
50 g/2 oz shelled walnuts, chopped	½ cup chopped walnuts

Oven: 150°C/300°F/Mark 2
Two 450 g/1 lb loaf tins, each measuring about
13 × 10 × 5 cm/5 × 4 × 2 inches
Makes 2 loaves

Butter the loaf tins. Cream the butter and sugar together, then beat in the eggs one at a time. Purée the bananas in a food processor or mash them vigorously with a fork, and beat this purée into the mixture. Sift the flour, salt and baking powder into a bowl, then beat them into the banana mixture, a little at a time. Stir in the walnuts. Turn the mixture into the tins and bake for 1¼ hours. Allow the loaves to cool in their tins for 10 minutes before carefully turning out on to a wire rack.

This moist bread will keep for several days in an airtight tin. It is lovely spread liberally with butter or cream cheese.

The Full English Breakfast

The English breakfast reached its full splendour in Victorian and Edwardian times. A sideboard was set in advance with cold meats and pies, and then the hot dishes appeared in silver chafing-dishes kept hot over spirit lamps. But let us allow the authentic breakfasters of those times to describe it in their own words. 'The tea consumed was the very best, the coffee the very blackest, the cream the very thickest,' wrote Anthony Trollope in *The Warden*, 1855. 'There was dry toast and buttered toast, muffins and crumpets; hot bread and cold bread, white bread and brown bread, home-made bread and bakers' bread, wheaten bread and oaten bread; and if there be other breads than these, they were there; there were eggs in napkins, and crispy bits of bacon under silver covers; and there were little fishes in a little box, and devilled kidneys frizzling on a hot-water dish—which, by-the way, were placed closely contiguous to the plate of the worthy archdeacon himself. Over and above this, on a snow white napkin, spread upon the sideboard, was a huge ham and a huge sirloin; the latter having laden the dinner table on the previous evening. Such was the ordinary fare at Plumstead Episcopi.'

In *Small Talk*, 1937, Harold Nicolson remembered the opulence of the *fin de siècle* breakfast table: 'Edwardian breakfasts were in no sense a hurried proceeding. The porridge was disposed of negligently, people walking about and watching the rain descend upon the Italian garden. Then would come whiting and omelette and devilled kidneys and little fishy messes in shells. And then tongue and ham and a slice of ptarmigan. And then scones and honey and marmalade. And then a little melon, and a nectarine or two, and just one or two of those delicious raspberries. The men at that stage would drift (I employ the accepted term) to the smoking room. The women would idle in the saloon watching the rain descend upon the Italian garden.'

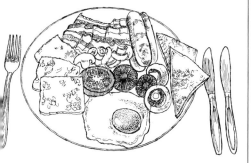

BACON AND EGGS

Bacon and eggs are crucial to the English breakfast. The bacon rashers may be streaky or best back, unsmoked or smoked, grilled or fried to the desired degree of crispness; the eggs may be cooked in any of a number of ways. Ham may take the place of bacon, sliced from a joint of home-baked bread-crumbed gammon. But in one form or another, bacon and eggs must always be there.

Bacon . . .

Smoked bacon rashers have a brown-gold rind and deep pink flesh. They keep well and their flavour is good, but they can be salty. Unsmoked bacon has a cream-coloured rind and pale pink flesh. The thinner the rasher, the crisper it will fry or grill. When you fry bacon, arrange the rashers in the pan so that they overlap with the lean lying on top of the fat of the rasher beneath. Reverse this arrangement for grilling, so that it is always the fat which meets the direct heat. Save the bacon fat which runs off during cooking; it is ideal for frying breakfast eggs, mushrooms, tomatoes and bread.

. . . or Ham . . .

A handsome joint of gammon or ham to carve into fine-grained slices is a delicious long-keeping centrepiece for a breakfast table. This recipe is very simple, but allow three days from start to finish as long soaking and baking are involved.

METRIC/IMPERIAL	• CUP MEASURES
2.7 kg/6 lb gammon on the bone, middle leg or corner	6 lb bone-in country ham
100 g/4 oz fine fresh white breadcrumbs	2 cups fine fresh white bread crumbs

Oven: 170°C/325°F/Mark 3

Place the gammon or ham in your largest mixing bowl and cover with water. Leave to soak overnight. Next morning, drain and re-submerge it in fresh cold water. Do the same at

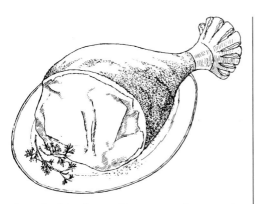

Give me a little ham and egg
And let me be alone I beg
Give me my tea, hot, sweet and weak,
Bring me The Times and do not speak

Bring porridge, bring sausage, bring fish for
a start,
Bring kidneys and mushrooms and
partridge's legs.
But let the foundation be bacon and eggs.

A. P. Herbert, *A Book of Ballads*

' "'Tis but simple fare," said Coningsby as the maiden uncovered the still hissing bacon and the eggs that looked like tufts of primroses.

' "Nay, a national dish," said the stranger, glancing quickly at the table, "whose fame is a proverb. And what more should we expect under a simple roof! How much better than an omelette or a greasy olla, that they would give us in a posada! 'Tis a wonderful country this England!" '

Benjamin Disraeli, *Coningsby*

the end of the day, and leave to soak overnight again. Drain it again on the second morning. This will have soaked away a good deal of its saltiness. Now wrap it in cooking foil, making sure that all the foil's edges are so folded as to seal the gammon hermetically.

Place the wrapped gammon on a rack in a baking tin half-filled with water. Bake for 3 hours. Turn the wrapped gammon over on the rack and bake for another 2 hours.

Remove from the oven, unwrap and leave it to cool for 45 minutes.

Toast the breadcrumbs on a baking sheet under the grill/broiler. Unwrap the gammon, and peel off the rind in one large piece. Press the toasted breadcrumbs into the warm white fat so exposed, wrap the joint again in fresh foil, place it in the large bowl with a weighted board on top, and leave overnight again.

The gammon is now ready to carve. It will keep well for a week or more if wrapped in clean greaseproof or wax paper at the end of each breakfast before being replaced in the refrigerator.

...and Eggs

SCRAMBLED EGGS

Ritz's great chef, Escoffier, considered scrambled eggs to be 'undoubtedly the finest of all egg-preparations, provided the eggs are not over-cooked, and they be kept soft and creamy.' He used to beat the eggs with a fork on whose tines he had speared a peeled garlic clove. This subtly strengthened their flavour.

METRIC/IMPERIAL	CUP MEASURES
4 eggs	4 eggs
30 ml/2 tbsp milk or single cream	2 tbsp milk or light cream
salt and white pepper	salt and white pepper
25 g/1 oz butter	2 tbsp butter
2 slices hot buttered toast	2 slices hot buttered toast

Serves 2

Crack the eggs into a bowl and beat them with the milk or cream and seasoning. In a medium-sized heavy-based saucepan, heat the butter until it foams, and swirl it around. Pour in the eggs and stir them with a wooden spoon over a low heat. Escoffier advised, 'Take care to avoid cooking too quickly, which, by instantaneously solidifying the egg-molecules, would cause lumps to form in the mass—a thing which, above all, should be guarded against.' Draw the mixture up in folds as the eggs start to grow thicker. Remove from the heat while still not quite cooked, and continue stirring—the eggs will be perfectly ready when you spoon them on to hot buttered toast 30 seconds later.

BOILED EGGS

The eggs should be at room temperature, and very fresh. Mrs Beeton wrote, 'Eggs for boiling cannot be too fresh or boiled too soon after they are laid.' Unless cooked in vast quantities, they should be boiled in a small pan so they cannot dance around and crack themselves. A further preventative against cracking is to pierce the rounded end of the egg with a fine needle before cooking. Bring a pan of water to a slow boil, and lower the eggs into it using a tablespoon and the utmost gentleness. Large eggs should be cooked like this for 3 minutes to soft boil them and $4\frac{1}{2}$ minutes for a soft yolk and firm white; small eggs need $2\frac{1}{4}$ minutes to soft-boil them and 3 minutes for a soft yolk and firm white. If your eggs are as fresh as Mrs Beeton advised, allow an extra minute on all these times. Eat them with a little horn spoon. Superstitious types smash the shells afterwards in case witches should make boats of them.

In marble walls as white as milk
Lined with a skin as soft as silk,
Within a fountain crystal-clear
A golden apple doth appear.
No doors there are to this stronghold
Yet thieves break in and steal the gold.

FRIED EGGS

Melt some bacon fat or lard in a frying pan until hot but not sizzling. Crack your egg into a cup, pour it on to a saucer, and from there slide it into the pan. Cook over a low to medium heat, making sure that the white does not remain jellified on top by basting it with the hot surrounding fat, or by placing a saucepan lid over it. The egg is done when the white is set but not hard or browned in any way. For those worried by thoughts of fat and cholesterol, here is what Della Lutes had to say in *The Country Kitchen*: 'An egg fried in this fashion, its qualities and virtues instantly sealed within it by a hot, sweet coating of honest fat, cannot be too great a tax on the digestive machinery. Numberless were the fried eggs my father consumed, and he bore up under them until well past his eighty-fifth birthday.'

POACHED EGGS

Poached eggs are only successful when the egg are really fresh—otherwise they collapse an disintegrate distressingly in the water. Test a egg in shell for freshness by covering it wit cold water. The really fresh egg will stay wher it is, but those unsuitable for poaching will ti or even, if ancient, float.

To poach your fresh eggs, fill a shallow pa with boiling water and add a dash of vinega Adjust the heat so that the water is somewher between gently boiling and powerfully sim mering. Break each egg into a cup, and slide from there into the pan. Leave to poach unt the whites are opaque. When done, lift each eg out gently with a slotted spoon and hold in th air to drain. Place in a warm dish and trim o any trailers with kitchen scissors. Poached egg can be kept warm in warm water if necessary.

*G*ood Company

Any combination of bacon or ham and eggs is well accompanied by some tomatoes fried in bacon fat with a dash of cold tea, and a few buttered grilled mushrooms, seasoned after cooking with salt, pepper and a squeeze of lemon juice.

CHASSE

This is a venerable country-house breakfast dish, very savoury and satisfying when served piping hot.

METRIC/IMPERIAL	CUP MEASURES
1 large onion (or 2 small onions), sliced	1 large onion (or 2 small onions), sliced
25 g/1 oz butter	2 tbsp butter
25 g/1 oz bacon fat or lard	2 tbsp bacon fat or lard
350 g/12 oz tomatoes, skinned	¾ lb tomatoes, skinned
150 g/5 oz slice of cooked ham	5 oz slice of cooked ham
450 g/1 lb potatoes, boiled and diced	1 lb potatoes, boiled and diced
salt and pepper	salt and pepper
50 g/2 oz mature Cheddar cheese, grated	½ cup shredded sharp Cheddar cheese
a pinch of mixed spice	a pinch of apple pie spice

Serves 4

Fry the onion until quite soft in the melted butter and bacon fat or lard. Chop the tomatoes and ham into small pieces and add them to the onion. When they are all nicely browned, add a dash of water to the pan and then stir in the potatoes. Season with salt and pepper and cook for 10–15 minutes. Just before serving, stir in the cheese and spice. This is good on its own or served with poached eggs on top.

DEVILLED KIDNEYS

METRIC/IMPERIAL	CUP MEASURES
4 lambs' kidneys	4 lambs' kidneys
salt and pepper	salt and pepper
50 g/2 oz butter	4 tbsp butter
10 ml/2 tsp made English mustard	2 tsp prepared English mustard
10 ml/2 tsp Worcestershire sauce	2 tsp Worcestershire sauce
5 ml/1 tsp mango chutney	1 tsp mango chutney
5 ml/1 tsp anchovy sauce, or 2 anchovy fillets, chopped	1 tsp anchovy sauce, or 2 anchovy fillets, chopped
5 ml/1 tsp wine vinegar	1 tsp wine vinegar
5 ml/1 tsp tomato purée	1 tsp tomato paste
5 ml/1 tsp salt and sugar, mixed	1 tsp salt and sugar, mixed
a bold pinch of cayenne pepper	a bold pinch of cayenne

Serves 2

Halve and skin the kidneys, and remove their central core. Slice and season them, then fry for a minute or two in the sizzling hot butter. Remove them from the pan with a slotted spoon to a side plate. Add the remaining ingredients to the butter and heat until the devil mixture bubbles, stirring all the while. Remove from the heat, stir in the kidneys, and serve very hot with toast.

BUTTERED BLOATERS

These silvery soft-fleshed fish were extremely popular with the Victorians. A bloater is a whole herring which has been caught close enough to shore to be brought on to dry land while still fresh (kippers, on the other hand, are usually caught further out and need to be salted while still on board). Once a bloater-to-be arrives on land, it is only very lightly treated with salt and smoke, which means that it keeps its appetising plump appearance (as opposed to the leathery look of heavily-smoked fish) but also that it will not keep for long. The best bloaters are from Great Yarmouth.

To grill or broil a bloater, cut off its head and tail, open it down its back, gut it, and spread it flat on a rack. Dot the spread bloater with butter and grill on both sides. Serve piping hot with an extra pat of butter.

BREAKFAST SAUSAGES

Commercial brand-name sausages often contain a great deal of rusk and water and not much pork. Unless you know of a good butcher who makes his own, it is worth the

time and trouble to try making sausages at least once. Remember that you will need sausage casings [available from some butchers or delicatessens or mail order (including export orders) from Gysin & Hanson Ltd, 9 Trundleys Rd, Deptford, London SE8 5JG].

——METRIC/IMPERIAL—— •	——CUP MEASURES——
450 g/1 lb lean boneless pork (shoulder, neck, leg or loin)	1 lb lean boneless pork (shoulder, leg or loin)
225 g/8 oz belly of pork	½ lb fresh side pork
1 thick slice of bread (25–50 g/1–2 oz)	1 thick slice of bread (1–2 oz)
10 ml/2 tsp salt	2 tsp salt
5 ml/1 tsp coarsely ground black pepper	1 tsp coarsely ground black pepper
5 ml/1 tsp *quatre épices* or ground allspice	1 tsp *quatre épices* or ground allspice
grated rind of 1 lemon	grated rind of 1 lemon
15 ml/1 tbsp chopped fresh sage and/or thyme	1 tbsp chopped fresh sage and/or thyme
15 ml/1 tbsp chopped parsley	1 tbsp chopped parsley

Makes about 700 g/1½ lb sausages

Trim the meat of gristle. Cut the meat and fat into cubes. Mix them together and either put through a mincer or meat grinder, or chop in a food processor for a few seconds only. Soak the bread in water, then squeeze it out and

break it up into a mixing bowl. Stir in the meat and fat, then all the other ingredients. Test whether the mixture is seasoned to your liking by frying a spoonful of it and tasting. Adjust seasoning if necessary.

Slip the sausage casing over a cold tap and run water through it, throwing away any sections where holes appear. Now certain lucky people will fix their sausage-stuffing attachment to the food processor. The rest of us will proceed to fill the casing with the sausage meat by cutting off a length and holding one end of it around the neck of a large funnel. Tie a knot in the dangling end of the casing. Now start pushing the sausage meat through the funnel into the casing, prodding at it with the handle of a wooden spoon. Twist the casing at sausage-length intervals. Do not fill too tightly or the sausages will burst when cooked. Hang them in a cool dry place for a day or two before frying or grilling/broiling them. Whichever way you cook them, cook them *slowly*.

If you cannot obtain, or shudder at the idea of filling, sausage casings, shape the sausage meat into sausage lengths, roll them in flour, and fry. For those who have sausage casing left over, sprinkle with salt and store in a large screwtop jar in the refrigerator until the next time you make sausages.

GLAMORGAN SAUSAGES

'The breakfast was delicious, consisting of excellent tea, buttered toast and Glamorgan sausages,' wrote George Borrow over a century ago in *Wild Wales*. These meatless Welsh sausages are a good alternative to the conventional English variety, both for vegetarians and for those who cannot face the skin-stuffing antics involved in sausage-making.

METRIC/IMPERIAL	CUP MEASURES
175 g/6 oz fresh white breadcrumbs	3 cups fresh white bread crumbs
100 g/4 oz Caerphilly cheese, grated	1 cup shredded Caerphilly cheese
30 ml/2 tbsp finely chopped leek	2 tbsp finely chopped leek
2 eggs	2 eggs
6 sprigs of parsley, chopped	6 sprigs of parsley, chopped
5 ml/1 tsp dry mustard powder	1 tsp dry mustard powder
5 ml/1 tsp each salt and pepper	1 tsp each salt and pepper
1 egg white	1 egg white
bacon fat (or butter, if vegetarian) for frying	bacon fat (or butter, if vegetarian) for frying

Makes 10 little sausages

Mix together two-thirds of the breadcrumbs with the cheese and leek. Beat the eggs, then whisk in the parsley, mustard and seasoning. Bind the breadcrumb mixture with the egg mixture, stirring well and adding a little water if it refuses to cohere at first. Make ten little sausage shapes, brush them with the egg white and coat them in the remaining breadcrumbs. Fry gently in bacon fat or butter until golden.

The Scottish Highland Breakfast

*S*cottish breakfasts are renowned for their heartiness. They raise weather-defying spirits against the day ahead and are so sustaining that they may easily serve as its main meal. Sir Walter Scott is among the country's most famous indigenous breakfast enthusiasts. Here, his biographer and son-in-law J.G. Lockhart describes: 'His table was always provided, in addition to the usual plentiful articles of a Scottish breakfast, with some solid article, on which he did most lusty execution— a round of beef— a pastry—or, most welcome of all, a cold sheep's head, the charms of which primitive dainty he has so gallantly defended against the disparaging sneers of Dr Johnson. A huge brown loaf flanked his elbow, and it was placed upon a broad wooden trencher, that he might cut and come again with the bolder knife. ... He never tasted anything more before dinner, and at dinner he ate ... sparingly.' In Sir Walter's first novel, 'Waverley found Miss Bradwardine presiding over the tea and coffee, the table loaded with warm bread both of flour, oatmeal, and barley-meal, in the shape of loaves, cakes, biscuits, and other varieties together with eggs, reindeer ham, mutton and beef ditto, smoked salmon, marmalade, and all other delicacies which induced even Johnson himself to extol the luxury of a Scotch breakfast above that of all other countries. A mess of oatmeal porridge flanked by a silver jug, which held an equal mixture of cream and buttermilk, was placed for the Baron's share of the repast.' Sir Walter was evidently extremely sensitive to the jibes of Dr Johnson, whose famous dictionary definition of 'OATS: a grain which in England is generally given to the horses, but which in Scotland supports the people' still gives offence today. Even Dr Johnson had to admit, however, that 'In the breakfast the Scots, whether of the Lowlands or mountains, must be confessed to excel us.'

SCOTTISH PORRIDGE

A true Scot will make porridge with medium oatmeal from Midlothian, spring water and salt. He or she will eat it smoking hot from a bowl, first dipping each horn-spoonful into another bowl of cold creamy milk at its side.

——METRIC/IMPERIAL—— •	——CUP MEASURES——
450 ml/$\frac{3}{4}$ pint water	2 cups water
45 ml/3 tbsp medium oatmeal	3 tbsp Scotch or Irish oatmeal
2.5 ml/$\frac{1}{2}$ tsp salt	$\frac{1}{2}$ tsp salt

Serves 2

Bring the water to a galloping boil in a heavy saucepan (or a cast-iron pot for maximum authenticity). Stream the oatmeal slowly from your left hand, sprinkling it lightly so that the grains are sealed separately as they meet the boiling water and do not have a chance to congregate in lumps. Meanwhile, stir the water with a wooden spoon; if you are a traditionalist, make sure that you stir it sunwise, and that your spoon is a spurtle or gruel-tree (wooden porridge-stick). Stir in the salt. Lower the heat and half cover the pan. Simmer for 30 minutes, stirring several times. If the porridge is too thick at the end of this, stir in a little boiling water. Add more salt if liked.

SASSENACH'S PORRIDGE

This is quicker and easier to make than the true Scots porridge, as it uses porridge oats or regular oatmeal, which have already gone through a steaming and rolling process to speed up their cooking time. Infant sassenachs write their names on the porridge's surface with a spoon of golden syrup held aloft. Salt is shunned; honey and brown sugar are the favoured seasonings, or, best of all, a sweet whisky sauce.

——METRIC/IMPERIAL——	•	——CUP MEASURES——
150 g/5 oz porridge oats		1⅔ cups regular oatmeal
800 ml/1⅓ pints milk		3½ cups milk
	Serves 3–4	

Sprinkle the oats into the milk and stir. Bring to the boil, and boil for 1 minute, stirring occasionally. Remove the pan from the heat and allow the porridge to stand for 2 or 3 minutes. Stir well before serving.

...AND WHISKY SAUCE

——METRIC/IMPERIAL——	•	——CUP MEASURES——
100 g/4 oz butter		¼ lb (1 stick) butter
150 g/6 oz caster sugar		¾ cup sugar
1 egg, beaten		1 egg, beaten
90 ml/6 tbsp whisky		6 tbsp Scotch whisky

In a heavy-based pan over a very low heat, stir the butter and sugar together until the butter has melted and the sugar has started to dissolve. Stir in the egg. Continue to cook the mixture until it thickens, never allowing it anywhere near boiling point. Remove from the heat and allow it to become tepid. Stir in the whisky. Serve this sauce in a little jug.

OATCAKES

These thin dry biscuits or crackers are made from water and oatmeal bound with a tiny amount of fat. They are delicious for breakfast with a cream or curd cheese like the Scottish Caboc or a Crowdie cheese. They are not the easiest biscuits in the world to make, and need practice.

——METRIC/IMPERIAL——	——CUP MEASURES——
100 g/4 oz fine oatmeal	¾ cup imported fine oatmeal, or Scotch oatmeal ground until fine
pinch of salt	
pinch of bicarbonate of soda	pinch of salt
10 g/¼ oz lard or bacon fat	pinch of baking soda
	1½ tsp lard or bacon fat
boiling water to mix	boiling water to mix
extra fine oatmeal for rolling out	extra fine oatmeal for rolling out

Makes 1 bannock or 4 farls

Preheat a griddle or large, heavy cast-iron frying pan. Mix the oatmeal, salt and soda in a bowl, and make a little well in the centre. Melt the fat in 3 tbsp of boiling water, and pour it into the well. Make a stiff dough, adding another tablespoon or two of boiling water if necessary. Sprinkle a pastry board with fine oatmeal and roll out the dough to a thickness of about 3 mm/⅛ inch. The Scottish way is to roll out a large round, which is either left whole (a bannock) or cut into quarters (farls). If making farls, trim their edges at this stage with a saucepan lid. Those who find it difficult to roll this dough into a good round will prefer to press out circular oatcakes from any-shaped rolled

dough using a 6 cm/2½ inch plain round cutter or teacup.

Rub the surfaces of the bannock, farls or oatcakes with more oatmeal to whiten them and prevent sticking. Carefully transfer them to the griddle or frying pan. Bake slowly until they start to curl slightly at the edges. Pale but firm, they should not be allowed to change colour. Do not turn them. Transfer to a wire rack, and store in an airtight tin sprinkled with oatmeal when quite cold.

A HIGHLAND BREAKFAST

'A highland breakfast: one kit of boiled eggs: a second, full of butter; a third, full of cream; an entire cheese made of goat's milk; a large earthen pot, full of honey; the best part of a ham; a cold venison pastry; a bushel of oatmeal, made into

thin cakes and bannocks, with a small wheaten loaf in the middle, for the strangers; a stone bottle full of whiskey, another of brandy, and a kilderkin of ale.'

Humphrey Clinker, Tobias Smollett, 1771

Fish for Breakfast

' "I don't know if you have ever noticed it, Jeeves, but a good, spirited kipper first thing in the morning seems to put heart into you."

' "Very true, sir, though I myself am more partial to a slice of ham." For some moments we discussed the relative merits of ham and kippers as buckers-up of the morale, there being much, of course, to be said on both sides.'

The Mating Season, P.G. Wodehouse

There would be no doubt in the mind of a good Scot as to the superiority of a kipper—or, come to that, a Finnan haddie or an Arbroath Smokie—over any English bacon flitch.

Finnan Haddie

Finnan haddies are haddock which have been cold-smoked using a clever method discovered in the village of Findon, near Aberdeen. As with kippers, avoid the dyed variety. Any bright yellow fish fillet claiming to be Finnan haddie is probably merely whiting in disguise, dyed and treated with smoke-flavoured chemicals. True Finnan haddies are pewter pale.

These delicious smoked fish can be eaten plain, grilled or gently poached in milk, and they are particularly delicious with poached eggs. Or they can be made into a more elaborate breakfast dish, as in the following recipe.

CREAMED FINNAN HADDIE

METRIC/IMPERIAL	•	CUP MEASURES
450 g/1 lb Finnan haddie, on the bone		1 lb Finnan haddie, on the bone
300 ml/½ pint milk, warmed		1¼ cups milk, warmed
30 g/1 oz butter		2 tbsp butter
15 g/½ oz plain flour		2 tbsp unbleached flour
150 ml/¼ pint single cream		⅔ cup heavy cream
cayenne pepper		cayenne

Oven: 180°C/350°F/Mark 4
Serves 2

Poach the haddock gently in the milk for about 10 minutes, then strain the milk off into a jug. Melt the butter and sift the flour into it, stirring well; then add just over half the haddock-poaching milk, a little at a time. Leave this white sauce to cook over a low heat while you flake the haddock's flesh, removing all the bones and skin. Stir the cream and fish into the sauce, and spoon this mixture into an oven dish. Cover, and heat through in the oven for 10–15 minutes. Sprinkle very lightly with cayenne pepper and serve on hot buttered toast.

Arbroath Smokies

Arbroath Smokies are particularly superior little haddock, unsplit yet decapitated, gutted, brined and hot-smoked over halved whisky barrels of candescent oak chips. They have midnight-golden skins and firm pale flesh, and are usually sold tied together in pairs.

They can be lightly grilled or broiled with butter, or heated through in the oven; or you can open the fish out before cooking it, removing its backbone and putting butter and pepper in its belly before folding it together again and heating it under the grill or broiler.

Kippers

A kipper is a split herring, strongly brined and cold-smoked. Many kippers are now dyed to a mahogany orange; you would be wise to avoid them. The finest undyed kippers come from Lochfyneside and Craster, and also from the Isle of Man and Great Yarmouth; they are a pale silvered gold in colour. Look for a plump kipper with nothing dry or brittle about it.

Jugged kippers retain their succulence, and are not quite as salty as grilled kippers; nor do they fill the room with pungent cooking smells. Fold your kipper in half and post it head downwards into a tall heavy stoneware jug. Pour in enough boiling water to cover it, and leave for 10 minutes. Drain and serve with a lump of unsalted butter.

If you are cooking a pair of kippers, clap them together around a knob of unsalted butter so that their skins face outwards, and grill or broil them.

THE SCOTTISH BREAKFAST AND THE WEE DRAM

A gross but common slander against the Scots is that they start their serious drinking at breakfast time, taking a nip of whisky along with their Finnan haddie. This may have been the case long ago, but as the following plaintive quotation illustrates, it was already on the wane in the eighteenth century:

'When I come to a friend's house of a morning, I used to be asked if I had had my morning draught yet. I am now asked if I have had my tea. And in lieu of the big quaigh (cup) with strong ale and toast, and after a dram of good wholesome Scots spirits, there is now the tea-kettle put to the fire, the tea-table and silver and china equipage brought in, and marmalade and cream.'

Mackintosh of Borlum, 1729

ABERDEEN BUTTERY ROWIES

These small flaky breakfast rolls are something like austere croissants.

METRIC/IMPERIAL	CUP MEASURES
450 g/1 lb strong plain white flour	3¼ cups white bread flour
30 g/1 oz fresh yeast	1 oz compressed yeast
15 ml/1 tbsp salt	1 tbsp salt
10 ml/2 tsp caster sugar	2 tsp sugar
300 ml/½ pint tepid water	1¼ cups tepid water
175 g/6 oz butter	6 oz (1½ sticks) butter
175 g/6 oz lard	6 oz (¾ cup) lard

Oven: 200°C/400°F/Mark 6
Makes 20–24

Sift the flour into a large mixing bowl and make a central well. Cream the yeast, salt and sugar in the tepid water and pour into the flour. Mix to a medium soft dough, and knead for 2–3 minutes. Cover the bowl and leave the dough to rise in a warm place until it has doubled in bulk, which will take a good hour.

Knock the dough down lightly on a pastry board sprinkled with rice flour before patting it into a large rectangle with the rice-floured heels of your hands. Cut a third of the fats into small pieces and dot them over the top two-thirds of the rectangle. Fold up the lowest third of the dough, and fold the top third down over it. Seal the edges by pressing lightly with a rolling pin. Leave to rest for half an hour in a cold place. Repeat this rolling, folding and resting procedure twice more, each time using another third of the fats and arranging a newly-folded edge to the side before rolling.

Now roll out the dough into a rectangle about 1 cm/½ inch thick. Cut it into squares of about 12 cm/5 inches. At this stage some leave the rowies as squares, while others like to shape them into buns by turning their edges under.

Transfer the rowies to two baking sheets dusted with rice flour, cover and leave in a warm place for another 30 minutes. Bake for 20–25 minutes until golden. Serve warm with creamy unsalted butter.

CLOUTIE DUMPLING

Although it can be served as an old-fashioned rib-sticking pudding with custard, this boiled fruity Cloutie dumpling is better adapted to modern tastes when it appears in its other role, sliced and fried with bacon at breakfast.

METRIC/IMPERIAL	CUP MEASURES
75 g/3 oz medium oatmeal	½ cup Scotch oatmeal, ground until fine
75 g/3 oz self-raising flour	⅔ cup self-rising flour
75 g/3 oz brown sugar	½ cup firmly packed brown sugar
75 g/3 oz shredded suet	⅔ cup shredded suet
2.5 ml/½ tsp bicarbonate of soda	½ tsp baking soda
10 ml/2 tsp mixed spice	2 tsp apple pie spice
50 g/2 oz currants	⅓ cup currants
50 g/2 oz sultanas	⅓ cup golden raisins
50 g/2 oz raisins	⅓ cup raisins
about 150 ml/¼ pint buttermilk	about ⅔ cup buttermilk

Serves 4–6

In a large mixing bowl, amalgamate the oatmeal, flour, sugar, suet, soda, spice and dried fruits. Stir in enough buttermilk to make a thick dough. Now take your pudding cloth, or clout, after which this dish is named, and dip it once in boiling water. (A large square of fine cotton makes a good pudding cloth.) Dredge the wet cloth with flour, and spread it out in a bowl. Roll the dough into one big ball, and place it in the centre of the cloth. Bring all the edges of the cloth together and tie them in a topknot with fine string. Leave room inside the cloth for the pudding to swell. Place a heat-resistant plate in the bottom of a deep saucepan and lower the dumpling on to it. Cover with boiling water. Simmer for 2½ hours, topping up with more boiling water whenever necessary. Cool and slice. Fry in bacon fat or lard. Serve with bacon and fried slices of black pudding (sausage made from oatmeal and pig's blood, a Northern delicacy).

The Continental Breakfast

The Continental Breakfast is simplicity itself, as long as you live within 2 minutes of a good Continental baker. If you are going to be making the croissants yourself, though, this type of breakfast will be a more complicated and precision-planned event altogether.

No plates are necessary for a Continental breakfast; you merely shake the tablecloth afterwards. Bring the baguette*, croissants or brioches or pains au chocolat to the table in a bread basket, accompanied perhaps by unsalted Normandy butter and a jar of *confiture d'abricots*. A pot of strong coffee and a jug of hot milk will stand by the broad breakfast cups and saucers or handleless breakfast bowls. In some fortunate households there will be hot chocolate too, as Colette described in this early morning scene from *My Mother's House*: 'the fire was already blazing, fed with dry wood. The milk was boiling on the blue-tiled charcoal stove. Nearby, a bar of chocolate was melting in a little water for my breakfast, and, seated squarely in her cane armchair, my mother was grinding the fragrant coffee which she roasted herself.'

*The long French stick impossible to make satisfactorily with other than French flour.

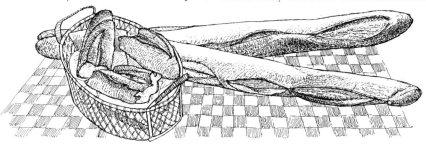

28

CROISSANTS

Good croissants are quite delicious, but they take 10 hours or more to make. In France, the fresh croissants at your breakfast table are the work of some baggy-eyed baker on night-shift. For the home cook, they combine the time-consuming demands of puff pastry with the extra complication of yeast. None of this will dismay the true croissant-lover, though it may serve to warn the breakfast dilettante that the creation of these pastries demands perseverance, dedication and cool hands.

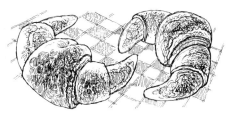

──METRIC/IMPERIAL── •	──CUP MEASURES──
225 g/8 oz strong plain white flour	1⅔ cups white bread flour
10 ml/2 tsp salt	2 tsp salt
150 ml/¼ pint mixed milk and water	⅔ cup mixed milk and water
25 ml/1½ tbsp sunflower oil	1½ tbsp sunflower oil
15 g/½ oz fresh yeast	½ oz compressed yeast
5 ml/1 tsp caster sugar	1 tsp sugar
115 g/4 oz unsalted butter	¼ lb (1 stick) unsalted butter
1 egg yolk, beaten with 5 ml/1 tsp water	1 egg yolk, beaten with 1 tsp water

Oven: 230°C/450°F/Mark 8
Makes 8 croissants

Sift the flour and half the salt into a bowl, then cover and place in a very low oven. Gently warm the milk and water, oil and remaining salt until tepid. Cream the yeast and sugar with a few spoonfuls of this liquid. Make a well in the middle of the warmed flour and pour in the yeast mixture followed by the rest of the liquid. Stir to mix, and leave for 5 minutes. Knead the dough until it is smooth and elastic, using a pastry scraper to help you.

Return it to a clean bowl, cover with a damp cloth and leave it in a warm place to rise until it has grown to twice its size. This will take up to 4 hours. Knead it lightly on a floured board for a minute before patting it into a rectangle about 30 × 15 cm/12 × 6 inches with the floured heels of your hands. Fold into three and leave the dough to rise again for about an hour. Now chill it for 30 minutes.

Roll out the cool dough on a lightly floured surface into the same-sized rectangle as before. Cut a third of the butter into small pieces and place them on one half of the pastry, leaving a 1 cm/½ inch border, and enclose by folding over the other pastry half. Seal the edges by pressing with a rolling pin. Turn the pastry round on the board so the folded edge is to one side, and roll out into a rectangle about three times as long as it is wide. Fold the top third down and the bottom third up and press lightly with a rolling pin. Wrap the pastry and leave it to rest in the refrigerator for an hour. Repeat this rolling, folding and resting procedure twice more, each time using another third of the butter, arranging a folded edge to the side before rolling, and reducing the length of each resting time to 20 minutes. At last, chill the finished dough for 1½ hours or until you are ready for the penultimate stage.

Butter a baking sheet. Roll out the dough into a 35 cm/14 inch square, and quarter this into four smaller squares. Cut each of these into two triangles. With the longest edge nearest to you, roll up each triangle in turn, using one hand to roll the dough away from you and the other to pull out the point. You should finish each roll so that the central pointed end is underneath, ensuring that it will not rear up during the cooking. In France, all-butter croissants are often left straight like this, while the curved ones contain other, cheaper fats. Having gone to this trouble, though, you will probably feel cheated if you do not now curve each roll into a crescent or 'croissant'.

Slide the croissants on to the baking sheet, arranging them so that the points of those on the outside rows are turned inwards (to prevent burning). Cover and leave them to prove in your warmest room or airing cupboard for an hour until they have grown to a good size.

Brush their tops with the egg glaze, and bake for 12–15 minutes until golden brown. Cool on a rack for 10 minutes, then serve them.

Unless you want to work through the night to serve these freshly baked at breakfast, you can leave the risen but uncooked croissants, covered, in the refrigerator overnight (taking them out a good half hour before baking them); or you can freeze them quite successfully (either risen but uncooked, or in their fully baked state); or you can go to bed leaving the dough to its last relaxation overnight in the refrigerator before starting the rolling-out and final proofing stages early next morning.

BRIOCHE

The steep-sided fluted brioche loaf is the richest, butteriest and airiest of all breads. Only cool-fingered cooks with a pastry marble should attempt to make it, and then not on hot days. The sunny-coloured dough must rise three times before it is ready for baking.

——METRIC/IMPERIAL—— • ——CUP MEASURES——	
8 g/¼ oz fresh yeast	¼ oz compressed yeast
25 ml/1½ tbsp tepid water	1½ tbsp tepid water
225 g/8 oz strong plain white flour	1⅔ cups white bread flour
7.5 ml/1½ tsp salt	1½ tsp salt
15 ml/1 tbsp caster sugar	1 tbsp sugar
2 eggs, beaten	2 eggs, beaten
50 g/2 oz unsalted butter, softened	4 tbsp unsalted butter, softened
1 egg, beaten with 15 ml/1 tbsp water and 2.5 ml/½ tsp sugar	1 egg, beaten with 1 tbsp water and ½ tsp sugar

Oven: 220°C/425°F/Mark 7
1.1 litre/2 pint/1 quart capacity fluted mould or 12 small fluted brioche moulds (standard size)
Makes 1 large brioche or 12 small brioches
(A large brioche will keep fresher and softer than small ones)

Cream the yeast with the tepid water, and leave in a warm place until frothy. Sift the flour, salt and sugar together into a large mixing bowl, make a well in the centre. Pour in the yeast liquid and mix well with a wooden spoon. Beat in the eggs, one at a time. Knead until smooth. Add the softened butter, a little at a time, mixing and pinching it in with your fingers until you have a soft paste. It may seem too soft, but do not panic. Knead it well by scooping it up in your fingers and slapping it lightly down on a pastry marble, lifting and slapping for a good 5 minutes until the dough is smooth and elastic. Use a pastry scraper to help if you find yourself in difficulties at this stage.

Turn this dough around in a lightly buttered bowl, and cover with a damp cloth. Leave it to rise at room temperature for about 2 hours or until it has doubled its bulk. Knock it down on the marble slab by folding it three times while patting it with floured hands. Once again place it in a covered bowl, leaving it at room temperature for 2 hours or so to double its bulk, then chill for 30 minutes; or leave overnight in the refrigerator.

Brush the brioche mould or moulds with melted butter. Knock down the dough once again, and knead until it feels springy and resilient. Cut off about a quarter of the dough and put it to one side. Now shape the remaining dough into a sphere or 12 small globes, according to whether you are making a large brioche or small ones, and place in the mould or moulds. Make a dint in the top of each brioche with your fingertips. Roll the remaining paste into an egg shape (or 12 egg shapes), and press into the prepared dint or dints, narrowest end down.

Cover and leave at room temperature for the dough's third rising. It will swell almost to the rims of the mould or moulds. This may take anything between 1 and 2 hours, depending on the warmth of the room.

Brush the egg glaze over the brioche or brioches, avoiding cracks in the dough and the edges of the mould. Bake a large brioche for 20–25 minutes, or small brioches for 8–12 minutes. Transfer to a wire rack immediately. Serve while still warm, alone or with butter or jam.

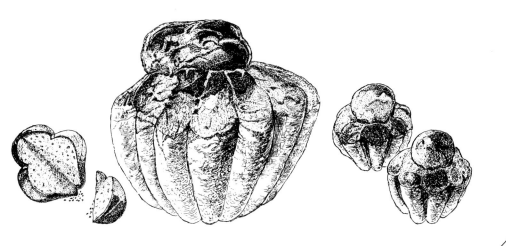

PAINS AU CHOCOLAT

These puffed oblong rolls of pastry enclose a central core of plain chocolate. They should be eaten fresh from the oven (even if that means reheating them at a low temperature for a few minutes) since each bitter-sweet heart should be just on the point of melting.

———METRIC/IMPERIAL——— •	———CUP MEASURES———
225 g/8 oz strong plain white flour	1⅓ cups white bread flour
5 ml/1 tsp salt	1 tsp salt
150 ml/¼ pint mixed milk and water	⅔ cup mixed milk and water
25 ml/1½ tbsp sunflower oil	1½ tbsp sunflower oil
15 g/½ oz fresh yeast	½ oz compressed yeast
5 ml/1 tsp caster sugar	1 tsp + 2 tbsp sugar
125 g/4 oz unsalted butter, softened	¼ lb (1 stick) unsalted butter, softened
125 g/4 oz plain chocolate	4 oz semisweet chocolate
30 ml/2 tbsp milk	2 tbsp milk
30 ml/2 tbsp granulated sugar	

Oven: 230°C/450°F/Mark 8
Makes 8 pains au chocolat

Sift the flour and salt into a warm bowl. Heat the milk and water with the oil until tepid. Cream the yeast and 1 teaspoon sugar with a little of this liquid. Make a well in the centre of the flour and stir in the yeast mixture followed by the rest of the liquid. Allow this dough to rest for 5 minutes. Now knead it lightly on a floured board until smooth and elastic, using a plastic spatula to help control the dough. Return it to a clean bowl, cover with a cloth and leave in a warm place to rise for 4 hours. Knock the dough down, and leave it to grow again for an hour.

Knock the dough down again, then roll it out on a floured board into a rectangle three times as long as it is wide. Dot half the butter over one half of the pastry, leaving a 1 cm/½ inc. border, and enclose it by folding over the pastry half. Seal the edges by pressing down with a rolling pin. Turn the pastry round on the board so the folded edge is to one side, and roll out into the same-sized rectangle as before. Fold the top third down and the bottom third up and press lightly with a rolling pin. Wrap the pastry and leave it to rest in the refrigerator for 20 minutes.

Repeat this buttering, rolling and folding process, arranging the newly-folded edge to the side each time before rolling. Wrap again, and chill for an hour.

Butter a baking sheet. Flatten the dough with your knuckles, then divide it in half, then half again, so that you have four pieces. Roll out each piece lightly, once only if possible, into a 15 cm/6 inch square of about 5 mm/¼ inch thick or less. Cut each square into two equal rectangles. Cut the chocolate into eight equal sticks and place one down the centre of each rectangle. Fold the dough around the chocolate just as though making a sausage roll. Place on the baking sheet. Cover and leave to rise for an hour in a warm place.

Bake for 15–20 minutes or until golden brown. Heat the milk and 2 tablespoons sugar until the sugar has dissolved. Remove the pains au chocolat from the oven and immediately brush their surfaces with this sweet glaze.

CONFITURE D'ABRICOTS
(Apricot jam)

——METRIC/IMPERIAL—— •	——CUP MEASURES——
1.8 kg/4 lb fresh apricots, washed	4 lb fresh apricots, washed
450 ml/¾ pint water	2 cups water
grated rind and juice of 2 lemons	grated rind and juice of 2 lemons
1.8 kg/4 lb sugar, warmed	4 lb (9 cups) sugar, warmed

Makes about 3 kg/6½ lb

Cut the apricots in half, through to the stone, twisting the knife-scored halves in opposite directions to separate them. Crack a dozen of the apricot stones with a nutcracker or small hammer, and pull out their almond-flavoured kernels. Blanch these kernels in boiling water for a minute, then drain and slide them from their brown coats.

Simmer the apricots, water, and lemon rind and juice in a well-buttered preserving pan or kettle for 15 minutes or until the fruit is tender but still retains some form. Over a low heat, stir in the sugar patiently until it has quite dissolved. Bring to the boil and cook rapidly until set, which will take about 15–20 minutes. Stir frequently to prevent sticking. Remove from the heat and skim. Stir in the pale kernels. Pour into clean warm jars and cover as described on page 59.

CAFÉ AU LAIT

Strong French-roasted coffee and hot milk in two separate jugs are poured at the same time into large breakfast cups or bowls. Some like their café au lait to be an equal mixture, others prefer three parts coffee to one part milk. It is important to make the coffee very strong, allowing 2 tablespoons per breakfast cup at the very least, being mindful of Eliza Acton's warning from over a century ago: 'There is no beverage which is held in more universal esteem than good coffee and none in this country at least which is obtained with greater difficulty. We hear constant and well founded complaints from foreigners and English people of the wretched compounds so commonly served up here under its name.'

CAFÉ NATURE

This is taken at breakfast time only by those caffeine-addicts who have signed over their nervous systems to the devil. Made from a high burnt-flavoured roast, allowing 1 heaped tablespoon of coffee to 120 ml/4 fl oz of water, it is drunk straight and milkless from demi-tasse cups.

The Celebration Breakfast

Breakfast's morning optimism makes it a particularly suitable celebratory meal. A generous breakfast presented with élan is a good way to observe birthdays, anniversaries, centenaries and all other red-letter days; it may also express congratulations, general felicitations or welcome after a long journey. It makes a cheerful coda to an all-night vigil of pleasure. It might serve as a literal-minded wedding breakfast after an exceptionally early ceremony (conventional wedding breakfasts are really lunches in disguise). Part of the rites of spring ought to include a general festive breakfast on the first of May throughout the kingdom. At any celebration breakfast there should be early seasonal delicacies and something unexpected: tiny wild strawberries, gold-on-crimson, in a bowl lined with green leaves; a handful of field mushrooms fried in butter and kept warm in a chafing dish; a honeycomb with warm bread. Elements of caprice and exoticism are essential here contained in this chapter are recipes for a Russian delicacy, a crimson Edwardian fruit water and a sixteenth-century summer porridge.

Last of all, take to heart Mr Beeton's sterling advice: 'Always have a vase of freshly-gathered flowers on the breakfast-table, and, when convenient, a nicely-arranged dish of fruit.'

FROISE

This very old word 'froise' was last seen regularly in medieval manuscripts. A froisey or frausey used to be a dialect noun in the west country for a small feast or jubilation. As far as anyone can tell, a froise is a kind of fried bacon-and-egg dish.

METRIC/IMPERIAL	CUP MEASURES
50 g/2 oz plain flour	$\frac{1}{3}$ cup unbleached flour
salt and white pepper	salt and white pepper
2 eggs, beaten	2 eggs, beaten
150 ml/$\frac{1}{4}$ pint milk	$\frac{1}{2}$ cup milk
4 slices streaky bacon, rinded	4 slices bacon
$\frac{1}{2}$ small onion, chopped fine	$\frac{1}{2}$ small onion, chopped fine
50 g/2 oz butter	4 tbsp butter
1 egg white	1 egg white

Serves 2

Sift the flour with a little salt and pepper into a bowl. Stir in the eggs, one at a time, then gradually add the milk, beating until you have a smooth batter. Leave this to stand while you snip the bacon into little strips. Fry these with the onion in half the butter until they have changed colour. Drain and put to one side.

Beat the egg white until it is stiff, then fold it into the batter. Melt the remaining butter in a small frying pan until sizzling, then add half the batter. Fry over a moderate heat until it is almost set. Now sprinkle the bacon and onion pieces over this, and cover them with a top blanket of batter. Cook for a few minutes more, then flip the whole cake over in the pan and continue to cook until the other side is browned. Cut into wedges and serve hot. This is good with grilled mushrooms and tomatoes, or even with asparagus tips.

BLINIS

These little Russian yeasted buckwheat pancakes need to be planned before their appearance, so prepare them the night before. Eat them buttered, each crowned with a ring of sour cream or smetana encircling a spoon of caviar or lumpfish roe.

METRIC/IMPERIAL	CUP MEASURES
100 g/4 oz buckwheat flour	1 cup buckwheat flour
100 g/4 oz strong plain white flour	$\frac{3}{4}$ cup white bread flour
5 ml/1 tsp salt	1 tsp salt
400 ml/$\frac{3}{4}$ pint milk	2 cups milk
15 g/$\frac{1}{2}$ oz fresh yeast	$\frac{1}{2}$ oz compressed yeast
2 eggs, separated	2 eggs, separated
butter for frying	butter for frying

Makes about 24 blinis

Sift the flours and salt together into a large mixing bowl. Warm the milk gently until tepid, and stir in the yeast. Whisk the egg yolks into this liquid, then stir it into the flour until you have a thick batter.

Cover the bowl of batter and leave it in a warm place for 2 hours. At this stage you can place a weighted plate over the bowl, and refrigerate. Next morning, allow the batter to come to room temperature. Beat the egg whites until stiff, and fold them into the batter. Cover the bowl and leave in a warm place for an hour.

Brush a griddle or heavy cast-iron frying pan with melted butter, and place over a medium heat. Pour on large spoonfuls of batter; they will hold their shape, and each little pancake should be about 10 cm/4 inches in diameter. When holes appear on their surfaces, flip them over with a palette knife. They will only take a couple of minutes each to cook. Keep each batch warm in a covered warm bowl in the oven, buttering each blini before placing it in the bowl. Serve with a jug of melted butter, a bowl of sour cream and a dish of caviar.

FLUMMERY: A SIXTEENTH-CENTURY SUMMER PORRIDGE

'To make a pretty sort of Flummery. Put three handfuls of fine oatmeal into two quarts of water, let it steep a day and night, then pour off the clear water through a fine sieve, and boil it down until it is as thick as hasty pudding. Put in sugar to taste and a spoonful of orangeflower water. Pour it into a shallow dish to set for your use.'

Dorothy Hartley quotes this in her *Food in England*, commenting, 'This is a pleasant light summer substitute for porridge, and pleasant also with crushed fruit and cream. A fair quantity can be made at once, as it will keep if boiled daily.' It is also very refreshing with fresh orange slices and a scattering of grated lemon rind.

SALMON KEDGEREE

A delicate sophistication of the original Anglo-Indian curried recipe using smoked haddock (see page 8), this version is made with flaked fresh salmon.

METRIC/IMPERIAL	CUP MEASURES
100 g/4 oz long grain rice	⅔ cup long grain rice
salt	salt
15 ml/1 tbsp lemon juice	1 tbsp lemon juice
50 g/2 oz butter	4 tbsp butter
275 g/10 oz poached, flaked salmon	2 cups poached, flaked salmon
60 ml/4 tbsp single cream	¼ cup light cream
white and cayenne pepper	white pepper and cayenne
2 eggs, hard-boiled	2 eggs, hard-cooked
parsley, chopped very fine	parsley, chopped very fine

Serves 2–3

Cook the rice in plenty of boiling salted water, and simmer until tender. Drain well, and stir in the lemon juice.

While the rice is cooking, melt the butter in a saucepan, then add and gently heat the coral flakes of salmon, the cream, a pinch of white pepper and half a pinch of cayenne. Chop the eggs finely and stir them into the rice. Amalgamate the rice mixture with the creamy salmon, transfer to a hot dish, sprinkle over some green flecks of parsley, and serve immediately.

BREAKFAST BROSE

This is a variation on the rich Highland concoction known as Atholl Brose, transmuting it into something more ethereal altogether, suitable for morning consumption. It is excellent with fresh raspberries.

METRIC/IMPERIAL	CUP MEASURES
40 g/1½ oz medium oatmeal	5½ tbsp Scotch oatmeal
30 ml/2 tbsp liquid honey	2 tbsp liquid honey
30 ml/2 tbsp malt whisky	2 tbsp Scotch malt whisky
300 ml/½ pint Greek ewes' milk yoghurt	1¼ cups thick unflavoured yoghurt, preferably ewe's milk

Serves 4

Heat the oatmeal in a heavy unoiled frying pan until it is toasted golden brown. Beat the honey and whisky into the yoghurt (that made with ewe's milk is creamier and far less sharp-tasting than other sorts of yoghurt). Stir in most of the oatmeal. Spoon into pretty glasses, and sprinkle over the remaining oatmeal. Serve chilled.

FRESH FRUIT KEBABS

These are very easy to prepare, but must be composed at the last minute. Only use ripe fruit, and serve the kebabs in a regular line on a long painted platter. This recipe's ingredients are not hard-and-fast, so vary the fruits according to what is available.

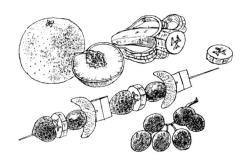

METRIC/IMPERIAL	•	CUP MEASURES
4 peaches or nectarines		4 peaches or nectarines
3 bananas		3 bananas
1 small melon		1 small melon
225 g/8 oz strawberries		½ lb (about 2 cups) strawberries
225 g/8 oz large black grapes		½ lb (about 2 cups) large purple grapes
juice of 2 lemons		juice of 2 lemons

Serves 6

Peel and slice the large fruits into big chunks, but leave the strawberries and grapes whole. Sprinkle the lemon juice over the fruit chunks and they will not lose their vividness to the air. Thread the pieces of fruit on to fine wooden skewers, paying particular attention to their colours, placing pale beside dark with the same care as you would if threading beads on to a necklace string.

Strawberries

Celebration breakfasts are immeasurably improved by the presence of strawberries—even out-of-season strawberries. Their colour, scent and deliciousness are inimitable. Do not wash them, but slice and sprinkle with sugar; or serve whole, *au nature*, leaving the prettiest examples unhulled, with little bowls of sugar and whipped cream for dipping. Arrange fresh good-looking specimens in a mound on a beautiful plate, with their green leaves tucked between them at intervals. Battered but flavoursome examples can be macerated with a little Beaujolais and left for 20 minutes before serving. Strawberries are refreshing when sprinkled with orange or lemon juice, as in Italy; they are also oddly delicious served with black pepper, chopped mint leaves and cream cheese.

A HINT AS TO TIME

'A breakfast party ends about the hour luncheons begin. Both hosts and guests have, therefore, ample time to recover their appetites, and to indulge in a quiet afternoon's rest, before the evening drive, and dinner.'

From *Culinary Jottings* by Wyvern

ESCOFFIER'S FRUIT WATER
(Eau de Groseilles Framboisées)

──METRIC/IMPERIAL── • ──CUP MEASURES──	
375 g/12 oz mixed red and white currants	¾ lb (about 2½ cups) mixed red and white currants
125 g/4 oz very ripe raspberries	¼ lb (1 cup) very ripe raspberries
600 ml/1 pint mineral water	2½ cups mineral water
175 g/6 oz caster sugar	⅞ cup sugar

Serves 4–6

Rub the fruit through a sieve with a wooden spoon into a large mixing bowl. Add the water to the juice. Stir in the sugar and three or four lumps of ice. Keep this mixture in a cool place for 20 minutes, stirring it from time to time with a silver spoon so that the sugar dissolves. Serve from a tall glass jug.

ICED MINT TEA

──METRIC/IMPERIAL── • ──CUP MEASURES──	
60 ml/4 tbsp chopped fresh mint leaves	¼ cup chopped fresh mint leaves
10 ml/2 tsp China tea	2 tsp China tea
900 ml/1½ pints boiling water	3¾ cups boiling water
50 g/2 oz caster sugar	¼ cup sugar

Serves 4–6

Spoon the mint leaves and tea into a warmed jug or teapot and pour the boiling water over them. Allow this to stand for 5 minutes, then strain into a glass jug. Stir in the sugar and allow to cool. Serve with ice and floating blue borage flowers if liked.

Tisanes

A choice of herb and flower teas should be offered at a celebration breakfast, separately, in a series of small china bowls. Made into tea, camomile flowers are good for the nerves, lime flowers are soothing, rose petals are wonderfully fragrant, sage leaves refresh the mouth and brighten the teeth, mint leaves are beneficial for those with digestive and hangover troubles, and marigold petals, while beautiful, have a bitterness which needs to be softened with honey. Do buy such teas from a good tea merchant where you can find the leaves and flowers still whole and recognisable. Beware the crumbled-up mixture of stale herbs often sold as 'Herb Tea'; only buy those beautiful desiccations which will uncurl and revive in their entirety in water. If you are lucky enough to find a glass teapot, you can watch the flowers expanding when you pour the boiling water over them. Only allow them to steep for 5 minutes before serving; that will bring out their fragrance but not allow bitterness to develop.

Buck's Fizz

This much-loved morning Champagne cup is a mixture of three parts of freshly-squeezed orange juice to five parts of chilled Champagne. Serve in tall fluted glasses.

Breakfast for the Modern Epicure

Breakfast is good for you. In literal terms, it is the meal which breaks your night's fast. When you wake in the morning, your body has been without nourishment for at least 10 hours. It is nothing but foolhardy, then, to dose it with black coffee and live off nervous energy for the next 5 hours until lunch-time. Your blood sugar level will fall and by eleven o'clock you will be wanting biscuits or cookies. You will be neurotic and apathetic. Making time for breakfast insures against such unpleasantness.

The recipes in this chapter are designed for the time- and health-conscious twentieth-century breakfaster. All of them contain either or both of those twin dietary paragons, fruit and fibre, and all of them are extremely quick and easy to make. Choose one from each group and you will have composed a deliciously sustaining breakfast.

Fruit

THE RITZ'S COMPÔTE OF FRESH FRUITS

In summer, strawberries, raspberries, and red, black and white currants cannot be improved upon in their natural state, eaten fresh and unadorned by anything but a light dusting of sugar. Other summer fruits like peaches, apricots, nectarines and black cherries can be lightly poached in a sugar syrup and served in separate bowls. The Ritz usually offers four to six varieties of poached fruit in summer (along with a selection of fresh fruits), increasing the number of these fruit compôtes in winter to eight or more. The advantage of keeping the compôtes distinct and separate is that each breakfaster can choose his own combination of fruits, producing a compôte tailor-made to his taste.

SUGAR SYRUP FOR FRUIT COMPÔTES

METRIC/IMPERIAL	CUP MEASURES
50 g/2 oz sugar	¼ cup sugar
600 ml/1 pint water	2½ cups water
a pinch of ground mixed spice	a pinch of apple pie spice
1 cinnamon stick	1 cinnamon stick

Stir the sugar into the water over heat until it has dissolved. Add the spices and boil hard for 5 minutes. Remove the cinnamon stick.

Add fruit to the hot syrup and cook gently for a very short while—ripe peeled pears, Mirabelle plums, fresh figs and white peaches may only need 1 minute, fresh hard black cherries 2 minutes, and apricots 3 minutes if very firm and slightly under-ripe. You must judge for yourself the ripeness of the fruit and the texture of its flesh, allowing the least cooking time to the softest and ripest and the most cooking time to the firmest and toughest. The time needed will vary from ½ minute to 4 minutes. Never over-cook, since the fruit will continue to soften in its heat-retaining syrup even after it is removed from the heat. Cook and serve each variety of fruit separately.

THE RITZ'S RHUBARB COMPÔTE

METRIC/IMPERIAL	CUP MEASURES
900 g/2 lb rhubarb	2 lb rhubarb
40 g/1½ oz sugar	3½ tbsp sugar
300 ml/½ pint water	1¼ cups water
150 ml/¼ pint white wine	⅔ cup white wine
4 juniper berries	4 juniper berries
a pinch of mixed spice	a pinch of apple pie spice

Oven: 200°C/400°F/Mark 6
Serves 3–4

Wash and skin the rhubarb, then cut it into 10 cm/4 inch pieces. Arrange it in a wide oven-proof dish. Make a syrup by dissolving the sugar in the water, stirring continuously until it boils. Add the wine, juniper berries and spice and bring to the boil again. Boil for 5 minutes. Strain this syrup over the rhubarb, and bake for 10 minutes. Cooked like this, the rhubarb will retain its shape and a little of its bite, and will not disintegrate into the livid mush of fibres which is its usual fate.

THE POPULAR COMPÔTE

A certain Lady Sysonby's culinary efforts were plagued by lissom slimming-crazy guests. However, she found a solution: 'I find compôtes are the great standby, and even the thinnest guest has been known to accept quite gratefully a whole stewed Bartlett pear, or peach, etc.'

Lady Sysonby's Cookbook, 1935

SPICED DRIED FRUIT COMPÔTE

Dried fruits are an excellent source of fibre and have a high mineral content. This is a good winter compôte to make when you are unable to buy fresh fruit.

METRIC/IMPERIAL	CUP MEASURES
100 g/4 oz dried apricots or peaches	1 cup dried apricots, or ⅔ cup dried peaches
100 g/4 oz dried figs	1 cup dried figs
100 g/4 oz dried apple rings	1½ cups dried apple rings
50 g/2 oz prunes	⅓ cup prunes
50 g/2 oz raisins	⅓ cup raisins
15 ml/1 tbsp jasmine, rose pouchong or other scented tea	1 tbsp jasmine, rose pouchong or other scented tea
1 cinnamon stick	1 cinnamon stick
4 whole cloves	4 whole cloves
1 strip of lemon peel	1 strip of lemon peel
600 ml/1 pint boiling water	2½ cups boiling water

Serves 6

Wash the dried fruits, then soak them in warm water for 2 hours or until they have plumped up. Place the tea, cinnamon, cloves and lemon peel in a bowl, and pour the boiling water over them. Leave for 20 minutes.

Drain the soaked fruits and spoon them into a saucepan. Strain the scented tea liquid over them. Simmer this mixture for 15–20 minutes, then remove from the heat and allow to cool. Turn into a cut glass bowl, cover and refrigerate. Serve the next morning. This is delicious with a few chopped walnuts or a spoon of Greek ewes' milk yoghurt. It will keep well for up to a week in the refrigerator.

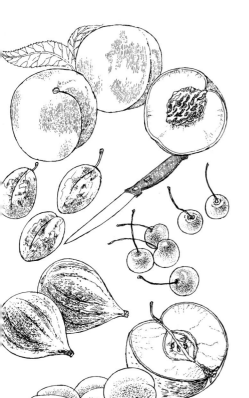

FLORIDA COCKTAIL

Serves 2

Take a pink grapefruit and an orange, and cut a slice off the top and bottom of each of them. Stand each fruit upright and cut off the peel and pith with a large serrated knife, slicing downwards all around the sides, following the natural curve of the fruit.

Prise the fruit segments apart over a bowl, then arrange them in two long-stemmed glass *coupes*, pouring over any juice collected in the bowl.

BREAKFAST EGG-NOG

This is the fastest breakfast of all to prepare, but sip it slowly because it is very concentrated and takes a little time to digest.

METRIC/IMPERIAL	CUP MEASURES
1 small ripe banana, chopped	1 small ripe banana, chopped
1 egg	1 egg
200 ml/7 fl oz skimmed milk	$\frac{7}{8}$ cup skim milk
juice of 1 orange	juice of 1 orange
5 ml/1 tsp honey	1 tsp honey
5 ml/1 tsp wheatgerm	1 tsp wheatgerm

Serves 1

Place all the ingredients in the goblet of a food blender, and whizz for a few seconds until the mixture is a pale sunny colour and frothy. Pour into a tall glass and sip slowly.

THE VANDYKED BREAKFAST GRAPEFRUIT

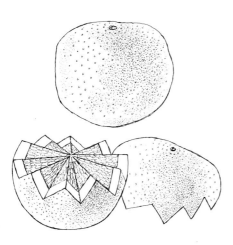

At the Ritz, the grapefruit are always pink. Take a grapefruit and a sharp little office knife, and, at a point a quarter of the way down the fruit, cut a zigzag line around the grapefruit hide. (This is called vandyking, after the regular deep-cut points on the clothes portrayed in the paintings of Vandyke.) Take off the lid formed by the top quarter of the grapefruit, and cut a 2.5 cm/1 inch wide niche on its summit. From the remaining three-quarters section, remove the core by further deft use of your office knife. Loosen the grapefruit segments by sliding a curved serrated grapefruit knife around just inside the skin. Now replace the grapefruit's lid, and stand a hulled upended strawberry or a Cape gooseberry (physalis) on its carved niche just before serving.

ibre

While attempting to avoid the visceral, it should be mentioned here to the health conscious breakfaster that oats are just what the intestinal tract most delights in. They are the basis for many of the healthiest and most satisfying breakfast dishes (including porridge of course—see chapter 3).

BIRCHER MUESLI

Dr Max Bircher-Benner, the pioneer of food reform, strongly believed in the curative powers of raw food. His Muesli, or Raw Fruit Porridge, was an adaptation of a centuries-old Swiss peasant dish, and became the standard breakfast served at his Zurich clinic (which was founded at the turn of the century). His patients so enjoyed 'The Dish' that they took the recipe away with them when they were

ured, and muesli has grown in popularity ever since. This is the original recipe, from which it ill be seen that Dr Bircher-Benner intended it include far more fruit than the modern uesli enthusiast generally adds. Also, a odern breakfaster may prefer to substitute oghurt mixed with honey for the condensed ilk in this recipe.

METRIC/IMPERIAL	CUP MEASURES
5 ml/1 tbsp rolled oats or coarse oatmeal	1 tbsp rolled oats
45 ml/3 tbsp water	3 tbsp water
15 ml/1 tbsp sweet condensed milk	1 tbsp sweet condensed milk
juice of ½ lemon	juice of ½ lemon
large apple or 2 small ones, polished clean with a dry cloth	1 large apple or 2 small ones, polished clean with a dry cloth
15 ml/1 tbsp finely chopped nuts	1 tbsp finely chopped nuts

Serves 1

Soak the oats in the water overnight. At breakfast time, stir the condensed milk and the lemon juice into the swollen oats. Grate the apple (or apples), skin, core, pips and all except the stalk, over the oat mixture, stirring it now and then so that the lemon juice stops the white apple gratings from discolouring in the air. Sprinkle the nuts over the dish, and serve immediately.

This muesli is delicious with extra soft fruits too, like apricots, cherries, strawberries and blackberries. But be sure always to include the apple first.

BREAKFAST CRUNCH

METRIC/IMPERIAL •	CUP MEASURES
175 g/6 oz rolled or porridge oats	2 cups rolled oats or regular oatmeal
50 g/2 oz desiccated coconut	⅔ cup shredded dried coconut
50 g/2 oz mixed shelled nuts, chopped	½ cup chopped mixed nuts
50 g/2 oz wheatgerm	½ cup wheatgerm
50 g/2 oz sultanas	⅓ cup golden raisins
15 g/½ oz sesame seeds	1½ tbsp sesame seeds
2.5 ml/½ tsp grated orange rind	½ tsp grated orange rind
50 g/2 oz soft brown sugar	⅓ cup brown sugar
150 ml/¼ pint water	⅔ cup water
150 ml/¼ pint sesame oil	⅔ cup sesame oil

Oven: 190°C/375°F/Mark 5
Serves 6

Mix the dry ingredients, except for half the sugar, together in a large mixing bowl. Whisk the remaining sugar into the water; add the oil and whisk again. Stir this sweet liquid into the dry ingredients. Spread the mixture over a non-stick baking sheet, and bake for 30 minutes, turning the crunchy pieces over now and then so that they toast evenly. Remove the baking sheet from the oven and allow to cool completely before storing in an airtight container. Serve with milk, yoghurt or fruit juice.

MODERN MUESLI

Rather than buy sugary commercial brands of muesli, assemble your own at home, varying the dried fruit and nut content to suit yourself. This muesli will keep for weeks if stored in an airtight container.

METRIC/IMPERIAL •	CUP MEASURES
225 g/8 oz 'jumbo' porridge oats	2⅔ cups regular oatmeal
225 g/8 oz rolled oats	2⅔ cups rolled oats
75 g/3 oz shelled walnuts, chopped	¾ cup chopped walnuts
75 g/3 oz shelled hazelnuts, chopped	¾ cup chopped hazelnuts (filberts)
50 g/2 oz dates or dried figs, chopped	⅓ cup chopped dates or dried figs
100 g/4 oz sultanas	⅔ cup golden raisins
100 g/4 oz dried apricots, chopped fine	⅔ cup finely chopped dried apricots
25 g/1 oz bran	½ cup bran
50 g/2 oz wheatgerm	½ cup wheatgerm
10 ml/2 tsp ground cinnamon	2 tsp ground cinnamon

Serves 10–12

Combine all the ingredients in the large mixing bowl you possess. Store in an airtight container. If you have an irredeemably sweet tooth, add 50–75 g/2–3 oz/about ½ cup of soft brown sugar to the mixture.

Eat the muesli with milk or plain yoghurt, or with a mixture of milk and freshly-squeezed orange juice.

QUICK IRISH SODA BREAD

This takes 2 minutes to make, then 40 minutes to bake. There is no yeast, no proving, and no waiting around. It is the easiest, quickest home-made bread in the world. Eat warm or cold, but at any rate within two days of making.

BRAN MUFFINS

These unyeasted muffins are a favourite breakfast delicacy in the United States, served warm, split and buttered. They are quick and easy to make, and carry their share of virtuous fibre.

——METRIC/IMPERIAL——	•	——CUP MEASURES——
100 g/4 oz plain flour		¾ cup unbleached flour
2.5 ml/½ tsp salt		½ tsp salt
15 ml/1 tbsp baking powder		1 tbsp baking powder
5 ml/1 tsp ground cinnamon		1 tsp ground cinnamon
50 g/2 oz bran		1 cup bran
15 ml/1 tbsp soft brown sugar		1 tbsp brown sugar
1 egg		1 egg
200 ml/7 fl oz milk		⅞ cup milk
25 g/1 oz butter, melted		2 tbsp butter, melted

Oven: 200°C/400°F/Mark 6
Makes 12 muffins

——METRIC/IMPERIAL——	•	——CUP MEASURES——
450 g/1 lb wholemeal flour		4 cups whole wheat flour
175 g/6 oz strong plain flour		1¼ cups white bread flour
50 g/2 oz fine oatmeal		6 tbsp imported fine oatmeal, or Scotch oatmeal ground until fine
7.5 ml/1½ tsp bicarbonate of soda		1½ tsp baking soda
pinch of salt		pinch of salt
600 ml/1 pint buttermilk		2½ cups buttermilk

Oven: 220°C/425°F/Mark 7
Makes 2 loaves

Mix all the dry ingredients together in a large bowl, and combine well. Pour in the buttermilk a little at a time, stirring as you go. Knead the mixture very lightly for a few seconds until you have a damp supple dough. Pull the dough into two pieces. Shape each lump into a rounded mound, broader than it is tall, and slash a cross in the centre of each with a large knife. Place each loaf on a baking sheet, and bake for 20 minutes. Now quickly open the oven, slip a deep cake tin over each loaf and shut the door before the oven temperature has a chance to fall; this will stop too hard a crust forming. After another 20 minutes baking, remove the loaves and cool on a wire rack.

Generously butter a tray of twelve deep bun, patty or American muffin tins. Sift the flour, salt, baking powder and cinnamon into a mixing bowl, then stir in the bran and brown sugar. Beat the egg with a fork; add the milk and melted butter, and beat again. Trickle this liquid over the dry ingredients, and stir only until the mixture is damp; do not mix it together to the point of smoothness. Spoon this rough batter into the tins until each is about two-thirds full. Quickly slide the tray into the oven and bake for 20 minutes. Ease the puffed-up muffins from their indentations and cool on a wire rack, or butter and eat them while they are still warm.

Breakfast Beverages

'There is nothing yet discovered which is a substitute to the Englishman for his cup of tea,' observed Florence Nightingale, and this is still true for millions all over the British Isles who are unspeakable before the first pot of the day. Breakfast teas are strong, bracing, usually Indian and drunk with milk. The United States and the Continent are more oriental in their approach, often favouring green teas and oolong, always hesitant about adding milk; there, coffee is generally the preferred breakfast beverage.

Coffee is less 'good' for you than tea since it is more violent in its action—one large cup of coffee contains 200 mg of the stimulant caffeine compared with the 65 mg in a comparable cup of tea. Coffee addicts quote Voltaire, who said, 'I know it is a poison, but it is a slow one.' Voltaire lived to the age of 84. Devotion to coffee stirs the voluptuary dormant even in the most ascetic soul—witness this paean fro[m] nineteenth-century American Congregatio[n]alist preacher and Temperance man Hen[ry] Ward Beecher: 'A cup of coffee—real coffee home-browned, home-ground, home mad[e] that comes to you dark as a hazel-eye, b[ut] changes to a golden bronze as you ter[m]per it with cream that never cheate[d] but was real cream from its birt[h] thick, tenderly yellow, perfect[ly] sweet, neither lumpy nor frothi[ng] on the Java: such a cup [of] coffee is a match f[or] twenty blue devils, a[nd] will exorcise them al[l.] Chocolate starts a d[if]ferent sort of day; a d[ay] against which there is no need [to] brace oneself, a day of insouciance Traditionally, chocolate was fam[ous] for its fructifying and aphrodisi[ac] properties: chocolate-drinking women look[ed] forward to producing twins at least, a[nd] Casanova drank it instead of Champagne.

48

BREAKFAST BEVERAGES AND THE BRAINBOX

COFFEE

'Coffee glides down into one's stomach and sets everything in motion. One's ideas advance in columns en route like battalions of the *grande armée*. Memories come up at the double bearing the standards which are to lead the troops into battle . . . the artillery of logic thunders along with its supply wagons and shells. Brilliant notions join in the combat as sharpshooters . . .' wrote Balzac. His persistence on the caffeine trail was described by his friend, the poet Gautier: 'His coffee was composed of three different kinds of bean. Bourbon, Martinique and Mocha. He bought the Bourbon in the rue de Montblanc, the Martinique in the rue des Vieilles and the Mocha in the Faubourg St Germain . . . I repeatedly accompanied Balzac on his shopping expeditions. Each time it involved half a day's journey right across Paris. But to Balzac good coffee was worth the trouble.'

TEA

'What should mightily recommend the use of tea to a gentleman of sprightly genius . . . is its eminent and unequalled power to take off, or prevent, drowsiness and dullness, damps and clouds on the brain and intellectual faculties. It begets a watchful briskness, dispels heaviness; it keeps the eye wakeful, the head clear, animates the intellectual powers, maintains or raises lively ideas, excites and sharpeneth the thoughts, gives fresh vigour and force to intervention, awakens senses and clears the mind.'

Discourse on Tea, Thomas Short, 1750

CHOCOLATE

'If any man has drunk a little too deeply from the cup of physical pleasure; if he has spent too much time at his desk that should have been spent asleep; if his fine spirits have become temporarily dulled; if he finds the air too damp, the minutes too slow, and the atmosphere too heavy to withstand; if he is obsessed by a fixed idea which bars him from any freedom of thought: if he is any of these poor creatures, we say, let him be given a good pint of amber-flavoured chocolate . . . and marvels will be performed,' wrote Brillat-Savarin in his famous *Physiologie du Gout* of 1825.

Tea

The strongest blends of tea are best at breakfast.

English Breakfast Tea There is no exact formula for this blend, but it is usually a strong mixture of small-leafed Indian and Ceylon teas, full-flavoured and invigorating, containing a large proportion of Assam.

Irish Breakfast Tea This is even more forceful than English Breakfast Tea, holding a higher proportion of Assam blended with a little fine-flavoured Ceylon.

Assam Forthright and mahogany-coloured when milk is added, this is the heartiest of all teas, full of malty gusto and other Victorian virtues. You may like to temper its Brahmaputra-Valley vigour by adding a spoon-ful of orchid-flavoured Keemun to the pot. On the other hand, if you want an even more vehement blend, stir in some Lapsang Souchong.

Lapsang Souchong This large-leafed tea has the flavour of woodsmoke and tar, supposedly owing to the particular soil of the Fujian Province of China where it is grown. Whisky-coloured and assertive, it is drunk without milk, particularly delicious with grilled bacon, smoked ham or kippers.

Ceylon Breakfast Tea This is less trenchant in flavour than other breakfast teas. A medium-strength tea, fine-flavoured and refreshing, it turns a pleasant golden colour when milk is added.

The Art of Tea-Making

Fill a tea kettle with freshly-drawn cold water, and bring this to the boil. Warm your teapot (glazed china or earthenware are best) by swirling a little boiling water around inside it, empty the teapot. Spoon your chosen tea from its caddy into the pot, allowing one heaped teaspoon of leaves for each person and one for the pot. Take the pot to the kettle and pour the boiling water over the leaves. Put the lid back on the teapot and allow it to stand and brew for anything from 3 to 6 minutes (less time for small leaves, more for large ones). Lay out the cups and saucers and, if you take milk in your tea, pour it into the bottom of the cups at this point. (The milk should always be cold.) Now stir the tea and pour it, using a strainer to catch the leaves.

Make sure you keep your tea in an airtight caddy or tin, as it readily absorbs moisture and other food odours.

Coffee

While breakfast teas are strong, the best breakfast coffees are mild and mellow, made from Light or Medium roast beans. The darker Full and High roast beans are preferred as 'after-dinner' varieties, and their insistent 'burnt' aroma is far less subtle and enticing than that of the breakfast blends.

GUIDE TO THE BEST
BREAKFAST BEANS

Arabica coffees (made from 'mountain-grown' beans grown at high altitudes) are superior to Robusta coffees (made from beans of a less flavoursome quality grown in lower regions). Robustas are cheaper than Arabicas, and are used to make instant coffee and most High roasts. Check the proportion of Arabica to Robusta in a blend with your coffee merchant; or, if buying pre-packed beans, look for a high proportion of Arabica. Any of the coffees described below will make lovely breakfast coffee.

Brazilian Bourbon Santos A good full-bodied coffee with clarity and natural sweetness.

Colombian Medellin Mildly acid, sharp and fragrant.

Ethiopian Longberry Harrar A spicy gamey taste, acid and fragrant.

Guatemalan Antiguas or Coban Full-bodied, fragrant, with a fine acidity.

Hawaiian Kona A rich, mellow, uncomplicated flavour with a fine aroma; grown on volcanic lava.

Jamaican Blue Ridge Mountain Some coffee enthusiasts say this is the best in the world. It is very hard to find, so buy when you can. Mellow and rich in natural sugars, also pleasantly acid.

Kenyan Peaberry This is that rare commodity, a coffee so well flavoured that it is unblended. It is particularly popular with the British. If you want to try roasting your own beans, ask for these spherical peaberries; because of their shape they are easier to roast evenly at home without specialist machinery. Shake them around constantly over heat in a frying pan until they reach the desired colour (not too dark).

Indian Mysore Fragrant and deeply-coloured, with a delicate velvety flavour.

Sumatran Mandheling A great favourite with the Dutch; very rich and heavy-bodied, but sweet and mellow too.

Venezuelan Caracas Blue Very popular in France and Spain; delicately acidic, mellow and winy.

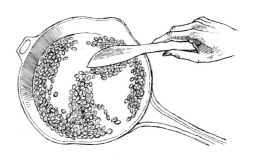

The Art of Making Coffee

There are over a dozen ways of making coffee, and each of them has its own loyal devotees. Whichever method you use, it is essential to the success of the brew that you grind your coffee beans to the correct fineness. Choose a hand-mill which can be adjusted to produce a wide range of grinds from fine to coarse; or, with an electric mill, whizz the beans for a short time for a coarse grind, longer for a fine grind.

Very fine grind: the paper filter method

BUYING COFFEE

Choose freshly-roasted beans and grind them yourself at home, grinding only as many as you need at a time. Fresh-roasted beans will keep for three weeks in an airtight jar. (Ready-ground vacuum-packed coffee only stays fresh for a week, even in an airtight jar, once it is opened.) Some people swear by the efficacy of storing freshly-roasted beans in the freezer, and grind them in their frozen state; this has the virtue of reducing the extra bitterness produced by the whizzing blades of high-speed electrical coffee mills which heat up the beans' oils. If you feel lazy and resort to instant coffee, freeze-dried varieties are most like the real thing, while the individual sachets of Italian espresso coffee sold in some delicatessens have the most flavour and force.

Fine grind: the three-part Drip pot; the Napoletana pot; the Moka Express or Espresso pot.

Regular or medium grind: the Cona machine; the jug percolator; the glass balloon vacuum method; the jug or cafetière.

The finer the grind, the less you need. Medium ground coffee is the least economical, but the brew is more fragrant.

Those who own specialist coffee equipment tripartite pots and funnels and balloons, will already possess the manufacturer's instructions on how to use them, and will be firmly convinced that their way is best. The simplest method of making coffee, however, requires no other equipment than a porcelain or earthenware jug, and produces excellent results.

THE JUG METHOD

Bring a tea kettle of freshly-drawn water to the boil. Warm your jug (or glass cafetière) by swirling a little boiling water around inside it; empty the jug. Spoon in the medium-ground coffee, allowing 2 tablespoons per large coffee cup (or double this amount for nerve-jangling demi-tasse strength). At any rate, there should be at least 6 tablespoons to every 600 ml/1 pint/ $2\frac{1}{2}$ cups of water. Do not skimp, or you will produce a weak and muddy mixture not worthy of the name of coffee. Now add a pinch of salt (some adventurous people like to add a seed from a cardamom pod, or a pinch of nutmeg or cloves instead). Pour on the freshly-boiling water. Stir with a wooden spoon, and cover. Leave to stand for 5 minutes. The grounds should have settled by now, but pour the coffee through a strainer anyway. (If using a cafetière, press the plunger-strainer down before pouring.) Add hot milk if liked.

*C*hocolate

Chocolate came to sixteenth-century Europe by courtesy of the last Aztec emperor, Montezuma. The cocoa nibs (ground roasted cocoa beans) were simmered for hours, cooled, skimmed of their buttery fat, reboiled with milk, thickened with eggs and flavoured with sugar and spices. All over the continent, converts competed to produce the best drinking chocolate recipe. Some 300 years after its arrival, a Dutchman named van Houten discovered how to squeeze the cocoa butter from the bean, and since then drinking chocolate has been much easier to prepare, and even more delicious. The long-lasting chocolate craze has inspired some of the prettiest porcelain ever made—little *tasses à chocolat* in Sèvres or faïence, gilded, scattered with rosebuds and mignonettes, poured from little flowery chocolate pots with wooden plungers. If ever you manage to secure such a drinking vessel, whether from an antique shop or your aged grand'mère, it will double your chocolate-drinking pleasure.

EVERYDAY DRINKING CHOCOLATE

Take 2 teaspoons of cocoa powder and mix to a paste with 4 teaspoons of cold water, then whisk the mixture into a pan holding a cupful of hot milk. Boil gently for 2 minutes, then whisk again if you like froth. Alternatively you can speed up the process by using instant cocoa or drinking chocolate powder, which consist of pre-sweetened pre-cooked cocoa. These dissolve easily in hot or cold milk.

PURIST'S HOT CHOCOLATE

——METRIC/IMPERIAL—— •	——CUP MEASURES——
50 g/2 oz plain or bitter chocolate, grated	2 oz semisweet or bittersweet chocolate, grated
600 ml/1 pint full cream milk, heated	$2\frac{1}{2}$ cups creamy milk, heated

Serves 2–3

Stir the chocolate into the milk until it has melted, then bring to the boil. Simmer gently for 30 minutes. Whisk for several minutes. Pour into cups from some little height, and a velvety froth will moustache the chocolate-drinker.

RICH SPICED DRINKING CHOCOLATE

——METRIC/IMPERIAL—— •	——CUP MEASURES——
100 g/$3\frac{1}{2}$ oz plain or bitter chocolate, grated	$3\frac{1}{2}$ oz semisweet or bittersweet chocolate, grated
600 ml/1 pint milk, heated	$2\frac{1}{2}$ cups milk, heated
1.25 ml/$\frac{1}{4}$ tsp ground cloves and 2.5 ml/$\frac{1}{2}$ tsp ground cinnamon, or 2.5 ml/$\frac{1}{2}$ tsp finely grated orange rind	$\frac{1}{4}$ tsp ground cloves and $\frac{1}{2}$ tsp ground cinnamon, or $\frac{1}{2}$ tsp finely grated orange rind

Serves 2–3

Stir the chocolate into the milk, and keep stirring until it has melted. Add your chosen spice, bring to simmering point, and whisk over a steady heat for 4 minutes. Some people like to whisk in an egg yolk just before serving. Others provide a stick of cinnamon for stirring instead of a teaspoon.

BREAKFAST MOCHA

Chocolate and coffee are delicious together, as this drink demonstrates.

——METRIC/IMPERIAL—— • ——CUP MEASURES——	
50 g/2 oz plain or bitter chocolate, grated	2 oz semisweet or bittersweet chocolate, grated
10 ml/2 tsp sugar	2 tsp sugar
30 ml/2 tbsp single cream	2 tbsp light cream
450 ml/¾ pint hot, freshly-made coffee	2 cups hot, freshly-made coffee

Serves 2

Melt the chocolate in a thick-based saucepan over the lowest possible heat, stirring and watching it the whole time. Stir in the sugar and the cream. Pour in the hot coffee a little at a time, whisking the mixture constantly as you do so.

Serve as it is or, if you like, with hot milk added to taste, or a spoonful of whipped cream for extra richness.

THE MORNING AFTER THE NIGHT BEFORE

This classic remedy, the Prairie Oyster, is so drastic that even a hangover may seem preferable.

——METRIC/IMPERIAL—— • ——CUP MEASURES——	
1 very fresh egg yolk, in its unbroken state	1 very fresh egg yolk, in its unbroken state
10 ml/2 tsp Worcestershire sauce	2 tsp Worcestershire sauce
2 shakes Tabasco or other hot pepper sauce	2 shakes hot pepper sauce
5 ml/1 tsp lemon juice	1 tsp lemon juice
5 ml/1 tsp malt vinegar	1 tsp malt vinegar
a pinch of salt	a pinch of salt
a pinch of black pepper	a pinch of black pepper

Serves 1

Lower the egg yolk into a small glass tumbler without breaking it. Stir the other ingredients together with a fork, then pour them over the egg yolk.

Shut your eyes, steel your nerve, and swallow the mixture whole, in one gulp.

DECADENCE AND DRINKING CHOCOLATE

There is something so frivolous about drinking this sweet extravagant beverage at breakfast that puritannical types have identified it with idleness and lax morals, and even (see the second extract) with political greed and decadence.

'J: "Pray how may you generally pass your time, madam? Your morning, for example."

'SJ: "Sir, like a woman of quality—I wake about two o'clock in the afternoon—I stretch—and make a sign for my chocolate—When I have drank three cups—I slide down again upon my back, with my arms over my head, while my two maids put on my stockings— Then hanging upon their shoulders, I am trail'd to my great chair, where I sit— and yawn—for my breakfast—If it don't come presently, I lie down upon my couch to say my prayers, while my maid reads me the play-bills." '

From *The Provok'd Wife*
by Sir John Vanbrugh

'Monseigneur could swallow a great many things with ease, and was by some few sullen minds supposed to be rather rapidly swallowing France; but, his morning's chocolate could not so much as get into the throat of Monseigneur, without the aid of four strong men besides the Cook.

'Yes. It took four men, all four ablaze with gorgeous decoration, and the Chief of them unable to exist with fewer than two gold watches in his pocket, emulative of the noble and chaste fashion set by Monseigneur, to conduct the happy chocolate to Monseigneur's lips. One lacquey carried the chocolate-pot into the sacred presence; a second, milled and frothed the chocolate with the little instrument he bore for that function; a third, presented the favoured napkin; a fourth (he of the two gold watches), poured the chocolate out. It was impossible for Monseigneur to dispense with one of these attendants on the chocolate and hold his high place under the admiring Heavens. Deep would have been the blot upon his escutcheon if his chocolate had been ignobly waited on by only three men; he must have died of two.'

From *A Tale of Two Cities*
by Charles Dickens

Marmalade

No breakfast table is complete without its pot of marmalade.

This is the story of how orange marmalade came to be invented in Dundee. One fine eighteenth-century morning, James Keiller, a merchant, was standing with a group of others at the quay in Tayside, when a Spanish ship unloaded a cargo of oranges from Seville. They seemed very cheap, and Mr Keiller, always a canny one for a bargain, bought the lot. 'You great daftie, Jimmy!' scolded his wife Janet, after tasting one of them in his shop. 'No wonder ye canny sell them! They're awfu' bitter.' A true thrifty Scotswoman, she decided to make the best of a bad job and took them home with her to see how they would do when boiled down into jam. They did remarkably well, with a bitter citrus deliciousness whose novelty took the city of Dundee by storm. The passion for marmalade spread like wildfire throughout Scotland, and from there eventually to the rest of the world. Everybody has their own favourite marmalade, whether sweet and amber-coloured or opaque and bitter, spiced with ginger, spiked with whisky, dense with chunky peel or of a crystal clarity supporting tawny shreds. Whichever you preferred version, it will nearly always be purer and less bland than a factory version when made at home. Mid-January to the end of February is the time for marmalade, for it is then that the essential bitter Seville oranges are in season. Making marmalade is a satisfying business, a colourful undertaking in the darkest months of the year, and makes the house smell wonderful.

THE TRADITIONAL MARMALADE METHOD

Buy just-ripe Seville oranges which look beaming, unblemished and bright-skinned. If you are too busy to make marmalade while Sevilles are in season, scrub them, pack them in freezer bags and freeze them whole, adding a couple of oranges extra to the recipe to allow for the slight loss of pectin caused by freezing. (Pectin is the secret setting agent they hold in their pith and pips.)

Arm yourself with: a preserving pan or kettle in flavourless thick-based stainless steel (aluminium, brass or copper are also suitable); a long-handled wooden spoon (hot marmalade is painful when splashed on the fingers); and a jam funnel or heat-proof jug. No other special equipment is required.

> 'Literary and other travellers used to be surprised and delighted with the tables liberally supplied with an appetite-provoking variety of fish, flesh and fowl, hot and cold; with rolls, scones, coffee, delicious cream, and especially with a condiment described by an old-time tourist, "a bitter-sweet but most delightful compound of orange skins and juices, called 'marmalade', which we never see in England".'
>
> *Memories of Books, Authors and Events,*
> James G. Bertram, 1893

Before

* Assign yourself a clear free afternoon in advance in which to make marmalade.

* Rub the base of the preserving pan with butter, which prevents sticking and reduces scum.

* Weigh or measure the sugar specified by the recipe and set it to warm in a very low oven.

* Wash, rinse and dry a number of $225\,g/\frac{1}{2}\,lb$ and $450\,g/1\,lb$ jam jars; invert and set them to warm on a large baking sheet in the plate-heating part of the oven, or in a very slow oven.

* Put three small plates in the refrigerator.

* Measure the water specified by the recipe into the preserving pan.

* Scrub the oranges and any other fruit mentioned in the recipe with a little brush. Rub dry with a clean tea-towel. Extricate and discard the small starry disc at each fruit's stalk end.

* Slice the fruit in half. Squeeze the juice from these citrus domes, pouring it through a sieve into the pan of water. The sieve will catch a quantity of precious pectin-filled pips and pith.

* Now take the hollowed orange shells and slice them with a very sharp knife into shreds, chunks or chips as specified by the recipe. Any scraps of pith and membrane still clinging to the rinds' interior should be added to the pips and pith in the sieve.

* Throw the chopped citrus rinds into the preserving pan.

* Loosely tie your collection of pips and pith together in a large square of muslin or cheesecloth, like Dick Whittington's bundle. Dangle this in the marmalade water by attaching it to the preserving pan's handle with string.

During

1. Simmer the mixture for anything between 1½–2 hours, until the liquid is reduced by about a third and the peel is translucent and tender when you squeeze a scrap between your fingers.

2. Remove the bag of pips and put it to one side to cool slightly. Pour the warmed sugar into the preserving pan, and stir with a long-handled wooden spoon over a low heat. Be patient and wait until it dissolves, or your marmalade will contain gritty crystals. To test whether it has dissolved, minutely examine the contents of the wooden spoon which you have dipped into the mixture; you should not be able to see any trace of sugar crystals.

3. Squeeze the bag of pips hard, so that it releases all its sticky pectin-rich juices into the marmalade pan. To do this, press the bag in a nylon sieve with the back of a wooden spoon; or crush it between two plates. Stir these juices well into the main mixture.

4. Bring the marmalade to the boil. The mixture will foam and rise in protest. In a short while the foaming will subside and scum will form at the edges. Continue to boil, stirring frequently to prevent sticking; after 10 minutes test for set, and at 3-minute intervals after that. (If you are using a saucepan rather than a preserving pan, the boiling will not be as fierce and so this stage can take up to half an hour to reach; take care that the marmalade does not 'catch' or burn during this time, by watching it and stirring it frequently.)

5. Test for set; if the marmalade has boiled long enough, it will set in the required manner when cooled in glass jars. First remove the pan from the heat, then try one of these test methods:

(a) Spoon some marmalade on to one of the cold plates taken from the refrigerator. Leave it for a few moments, then nudge it with the side of your finger. If a skin has formed which wrinkles when you prod the marmalade, then it is ready.

(b) Mix a cooled teaspoon of the mixture with 1 tablespoon of methylated spirits or alcohol. Leave for a minute. If it forms one or two large blobs, then the marmalade is ready. If it breaks into more than three blobs, return the pan to the boil.

Afterwards

* As soon as set point has been reached, remove the pan from the heat and skim scum from the marmalade's surface.

* Allow the marmalade to cool for 15 minutes, then stir it. This prevents the peel from congregating at the top of the jars.

* Stand the prepared jars close together on folded newspaper on a tray. Using a jam funnel or jug, pour marmalade into each of the jars

until 5 mm/¼ inch from the rim (the marmalade will shrink slightly as it grows cold). Wipe the sides and rims of the jars with a hot damp cloth until splash-free. Place a waxed paper disc waxed side down over the surface of the marmalade; press it gently so no air bubbles lurk. Leave until cold, then cover with cellophane circles moistened on the outside, held tautly in place by rubber bands. Alternatively, seal the marmalade's surface by pouring over a little liquid paraffin and allowing it to set in a thin film.

If the marmalade might be stored in conditions warmer than 10°C/50°F, it is a good idea to sterilise the seals to prevent mould and other spoilage occurring. To do this, fill hot jars with boiling hot marmalade, leaving 1 cm/½ inch headroom, wipe clean and seal at once, with screwband lids or metal caps. Immerse the jars in a large pan of boiling water; the water level should be 5 cm/2 inches above the tops of the jars. Boil for 10 minutes, then remove the jars and cool. Only use jars with airtight seals, that can withstand the heat of the boiling water.

When it is quite cold, stick on identifying hand-written labels with the marmalade's name and the date.

CLASSIC SEVILLE MARMALADE

—METRIC/IMPERIAL—	•	—CUP MEASURES—
1.4 kg/3 lb Seville oranges		3 lb Seville oranges
juice of 2 lemons		juice of 2 lemons
3.4 litres/6 pints water		3½ quarts water
2.7 kg/6 lb granulated or preserving sugar		6 lb (13½ cups) sugar

Makes about 4.5 kg/10 lb

This is an exemplary marmalade, the model upon which all other variations are based, and the best first choice for a marmalade-making novice. Follow the traditional method described above, slicing the orange peel· into 2.5 cm/1 inch-long strips twice the width of a matchstick.

COARSE-CUT SPANISH MARMALADE

—METRIC/IMPERIAL—	•	—CUP MEASURES—
1.4 kg/3 lb Seville oranges, scrubbed and discs removed		3 lb Seville oranges, scrubbed and discs removed
2.8 litres/5 pints water		3 quarts water
2.7 kg/6 lb granulated or preserving sugar		6 lb (13½ cups) sugar
juice of 2 large lemons		juice of 2 large lemons

Makes about 4 kg/9 lb

This recipe follows the 'whole fruit' method. It will appeal to those impetuous types who like to plunge straight in without preparation. It is particularly suitable for oranges which have been frozen (see page 57), and also when Sevilles are smaller and juicier than usual.

Simmer the whole oranges in 2.3 litres/

4 pints/5 pints of the water for 1½–2 hours in a covered preserving pan, until their orange coats are easily pierced with a fork. Lift them from the water with a slotted spoon and allow to cool until they reach a temperature which does not burn your hands. Cut them in half and scoop out their softened interiors of pips and pith with a teaspoon into a small saucepan. Add the remaining water to this pan, bring to the boil, and simmer for 15 minutes. While you wait, slice the peel into bold diagonal shards roughly 1.5 cm/⅝ inch wide and 3 cm/1¼ inches long. You cannot be as precise here as when using the traditional method, since the peel is soggier and less obedient. Some people simply cut it up roughly with a knife and fork. Return the peel to the first preserving pan of water. Add the sugar (warmed first if possible), the lemon juice, and the pectin-rich water strained through a sieve from the second little pan's pith and pips.

Stir with a long-handled wooden spoon over a low heat until the sugar has quite dissolved. Bring to the boil and proceed as described in the traditional method, from step 4 (page 58).

FLAME SHRED MARMALADE

METRIC/IMPERIAL	CUP MEASURES
900 g/2 lb Seville oranges, washed	2 lb Seville oranges, washed
2.6 litres/4½ pints water	11¼ cups water
juice of 2 lemons	juice of 2 lemons
1.4 kg/3 lb granulated or preserving sugar	3 lb (6¾ cups) sugar

Makes about 2.3 kg/5 lb

This is a clear auburn jelly flecked with citrin shreds of peel. It has been hailed as an evolu tionary improvement by those refined soul who cannot tolerate the characteristic bitter ness and chunky peel of traditional Sevill marmalade.

Peel the oranges superficially, taking care no to graze the white pith, until you have 100 g 4 oz of peel. Cut this into fine gold splinter with a sharp knife, and simmer in a small pan i 600 ml/1 pint/2½ cups of the water for about 1 hours. Meanwhile, roughly chop the rest of th fruit and simmer it in a covered preserving pa with 1.5 litres/2½ pints/1½ quarts of the water fo about 2 hours.

Drain the liquid from the orange shreds an put them carefully to one side. Add the draine liquid to the contents of the preserving pan. Ti a jelly bag or cloth at each corner to the legs o an upturned stool, and position a large bow beneath the cloth. Pour the contents of th preserving pan into the jelly cloth and allow t drip through into the bowl beneath for 1 minutes only. Tip the pulp remaining in th jelly bag back into the pan and add the last c the water. Simmer for 30 minutes, then pou the mixture back into the jelly bag and leave it to drip for at least 4 hours.

Stir together the two sets of liquid strained consecutively like this through the jelly bag. Test for pectin using method 5(b) as described on page 58. If it fails the test, reduce it by rapid boiling for 5 minutes, then test again.

Stir in the warmed sugar over a low heat until it has dissolved. At this stage, add the reserved cold shreds of peel. Bring to the boil and proceed from this point as described in the traditional method, from step 4 (page 58).

YE OLDE ENGLISH MARMALADE

——METRIC/IMPERIAL—— •	——CUP MEASURES——
900 g/2 lb Seville oranges	2 lb Seville oranges
2.3 litres/4 pints water	5 pints water
1.8 kg/4 lb granulated or preserving sugar	4 lb (9 cups) sugar
30 ml/2 rounded tbsp black treacle or molasses	2 rounded tbsp dark molasses

Makes about 2.7 kg/6 lb

A more honest name for this dark pungently-flavoured variety would be Apocryphal Marmalade, since it first appeared in 1901, long after most other marmalades.

Follow the traditional method, cutting the peel quite coarsely and adding the black treacle or molasses when you stir in the warmed sugar.

OXFORD MARMALADE

——METRIC/IMPERIAL—— •	——CUP MEASURES——
1.4 kg/3 lb Seville oranges	3 lb Seville oranges
3.4 litres/6 pints water	7½ pints water
2.7 kg/6 lb granulated or preserving sugar	6 lb (13½ cups) sugar

Makes about 4.5 kg/10 lb

This is the first variety of marmalade to be made in England. Marmalade crossed the border from Scotland quite late in Queen Victoria's reign; a gourmand don who had been visiting in Perthshire managed to smuggle its recipe back down to Oxford, where he gave it to Mrs Frank Cooper, his grocer's wife. She made several batches and it proved wildly popular with the undergraduates who, in their scholarly way, christened it 'squish'. Oxford marmalade is dark, sharp and strong-tasting.

Peel the oranges, and cut the resultant curlicues into strips. Chop the fruit up, extricating all the pips and putting them to one side in a little pile. Pile the chopped fruit flesh and sliced peel into a large bowl. Boil the water, then pour 600 ml/1 pint/2½ cups over the pips and the rest into the large bowl. Cover both bowls and leave overnight.

Now the pips will be coated in valuable transparent jelly. Carry them gently from the water in a slotted spoon to a nylon sieve. Sluice the pips' jelly into the large bowl by slowly pouring the water in which they have soaked over them. Drain the liquid from the large bowl into a jug, and pour it all back into the large bowl via the nylon sieve and over the pips. Throw away the now-exhausted pips.

Transfer the contents of the bowl to a large preserving pan and boil until the peel is quite tender. Long boiling gives the marmalade its desired darkness.

Remove the pan from the heat and stir in the sugar until it has utterly dissolved. Boil as gently as possible until the marmalade acquires an even tawnier depth of colour, and then boil rapidly for 15 minutes. Proceed from this point as described in the traditional method, from step 4 (page 58).

GINGER MARMALADE

——METRIC/IMPERIAL——	——CUP MEASURES——
1.4 kg/3 lb Seville oranges	3 lb Seville oranges
juice of 2 lemons	juice of 2 lemons
3.4 litres/6 pints water	7½ pints water
2.7 kg/6 lb granulated or preserving sugar	6 lb (13½ cups) sugar
50 g/2 oz knob of fresh root ginger, chopped and bruised	2 oz piece of fresh ginger root, chopped and bruised
125 g/4 oz crystallised or preserved ginger, washed and finely chopped	½ cup finely chopped, washed crystallised or preserved ginger

Makes about 4.5 kg/10 lb

Good for those who find it hard to wake up, this marmalade possesses an unusual heat and subtlety.

Follow the traditional method, tying the bruised root ginger into the muslin bag with the pips and pith. Once the marmalade has reached set point and been skimmed, stir in the crystallised or preserved ginger; then cool and pot as usual.

SWEET ST CLEMENT'S MARMALADE

—METRIC/IMPERIAL— • —CUP MEASURES—

sweet oranges, washed and thinly sliced	2 sweet oranges, washed and thinly sliced
3 lemons, washed and thinly sliced	3 lemons, washed and thinly sliced
.4 litres/2½ pints water	1½ quarts water
00 g/2 lb granulated or preserving sugar	2 lb (4½ cups) sugar

Makes about 1.8 kg/4 lb

his is a pleasant marmalade to make when
eville oranges are out of season.

Remove the pips from the oranges and
mons, and tie in a square of muslin or cheese-
oth. Follow the traditional method from the
iddle stage ('During', page 58).

ORANGE AND WHISKY MARMALADE

—METRIC/IMPERIAL— • —CUP MEASURES—

1.4 kg/3 lb Seville oranges	3 lb Seville oranges
juice of 2 lemons	juice of 2 lemons
3.4 litres/6 pints water	7½ pints water
7 kg/6 lb granulated or preserving sugar	6 lb (13½ cups) sugar
150 ml/¼ pint whisky	⅔ cup Scotch whisky

Makes about 4.5 kg/10 lb

his is an acquired taste, and possibly it is wiser
ot to acquire it unless you decide to use it
nce in a while as your own version of the Hair
f the Dog.

Follow the traditional method, stirring in the
hisky after you have removed the pan from
e heat when set point has been reached.

WINGED CHARIOT MARMALADE

Winged Chariot
Marmalade

—METRIC/IMPERIAL— • —CUP MEASURES—

1.4 kg/3 lb Seville oranges	3 lb Seville oranges
2 large lemons	2 large lemons
1.7 litres/3 pints water	7½ cups water
2.7 kg/6 lb granulated or preserving sugar	6 lb (13½ cups) sugar

Makes about 4.5 kg/10 lb

This recipe halves the time it usually takes to
make marmalade by using a pressure cooker to
soften the peel.

Prepare the fruit and muslin bag of pips and
pith following the traditional method. Slice the
orange peel thinly. Into the pressure cooker tip
the peel, fruit juices, muslin bag and half the
water. Bring to medium (10 lb) pressure and
cook for 20 minutes. Leave to cool.

Squeeze the juices from the muslin bag back
into the rest of the juice in the pressure cooker.
Add the remaining water and the sugar, stirring
until the sugar has dissolved. After this,
proceed as usual, boiling rapidly for 15 minutes
until set point has been reached, and so on.

Index